LIVING EXPATATIONS

The Journey of Repatriation

by:
Amy Perrier-Morin

Book cover design by:
Elisa

Published by:
Lotus & Haute L.L.C.

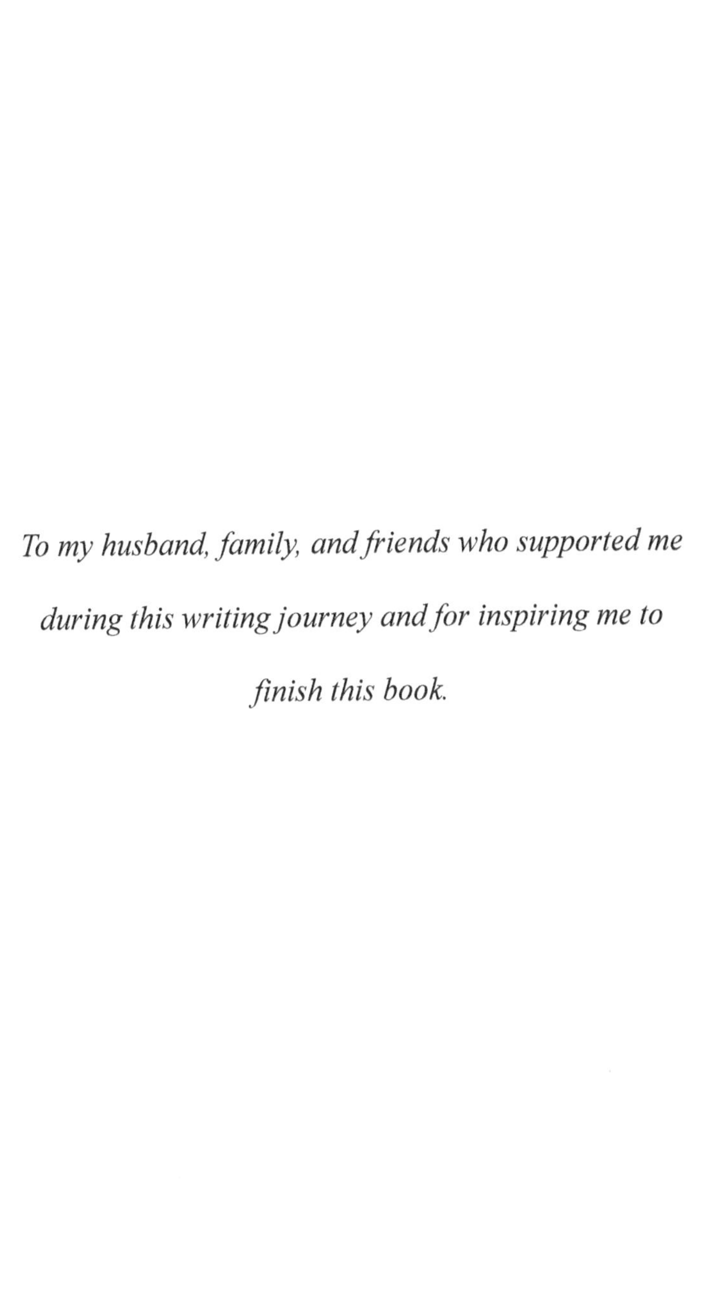

To my husband, family, and friends who supported me during this writing journey and for inspiring me to finish this book.

Foreword

The idea for this book came to me a few months after arriving in the United States. I visited my family up north over the Thanksgiving holiday and decided to start writing about all my repatriation experiences thus far.

I faced many situations when I arrived back in the States and thought how exciting it would be to ask other people for their stories and add them to this book. Then, I contacted as many people as possible to ask about their reverse culture shock experiences.

As you read this book, you might recognize echoes of your journey, whether you've ventured far from home or encountered the complexities of your new home. Others had experienced the same sense of alienation, the pangs of nostalgia mixed with longing for the life they had created abroad. Our stories have the same common thread, and these stories could resonate with anyone who has ever returned home after being overseas.

These words and stories I wrote, in hopes to offer a source of comfort that reverse culture shock is valid and a shared experience for us all.

Table of Contents

Chapter 1

Welcome Back Home!

"Coming home? Where do I even begin? It was beyond scary. Ultimately, the reality of it was scarier than the truth of coming home. Things here in the U.S. were portrayed much worse than they were here. The news sources made it seem like America had become filled with mania except for a few token people. As you know, I am a single woman in my 40s who has voluntarily remained that way. So some things I say may not be true for those with families, spouses, etc. In a way, I don't know which would be easier because I can see positives and disadvantages to both."

-Anne, who lived abroad for eleven years.

I wasn't ready. Physically and mentally. No one is before a life-changing move. I moved three times within the same country over the last three years, and now we are taking a more significant step by moving back home from overseas. Why was I having these butterflies fluttering all around my stomach? I was moving back to my own country, where I lived for twenty-six years. After living overseas for the last seven years, life slapped me in the face, and it was time for me to move on to the next chapter. As we landed at John F. Kennedy International Airport, it clicked why moving back home would be a shock. What a hot mess we were going through, and it was only the halfway point of our trip back to the United States, which I will get back to later in this book.

Moving is one of the top stressors a person can experience, along with death, divorce, job loss, and illness. I have had experiences with all of these, but thankfully, I was able to learn, cope, and grieve but mainly I never forgot to count my blessings. But moving houses, states, and, most of all, countries is stressful. I don't have kids, but I couldn't imagine the stress of moving with kids during the transition.

Pets, love them. I couldn't live without my two cats, but moving them was not fun! One of my cats has severe anxiety, much like his mom, and he doesn't travel well. He also senses when I am heading on a trip. Partially, it's my fault because I have traveled during almost every break I had in my host country. After all, the opportunities were there. So, whenever my cat saw a suitcase, he hid and turned his nose up at me. Trying to get him into a carrier, I usually have scratches all over my arms. He gave me the payback, and let's say I didn't get a good night's sleep for the next few nights. He got his revenge.

How could I forget? I didn't introduce myself. My name is Amy, and I wrote this book to tell you about the experiences I have had overseas and what my first two years were like moving back home to the United States. This book is used for entertainment purposes *only*. This book may not be for you or you may not fully understand the perspective if you have only lived in your home country, including the United States. However, keep reading if you want a good chuckle and read some fun experiences about my reverse culture shock and other stories people have shared as they repatriated back home. I also wrote this book as a guide to help Americans with some tips that helped me and others during the transition. For overseas Americans, I encourage you to pick up this book in case you're preparing to move back to the U.S. You still have the book in your hand or on an electronic device, correct? If so, good. Let's continue.

Also, my fun book is not to bash or bad mouth anyone but to give an overall sense of how I felt when moving back to my own country, which can sometimes feel foreign, even after two years of being here. Many would think that moving back to your home country is easy, but it's quite the opposite. Yeah, it's glorious to come back, see family and friends, drive to your favorite places, eat at the restaurants you've missed, and be familiar with your native language, but returning to your old world is different. Some things in America are the same, while things have changed, and then you still have to readjust, just like getting accustomed to a new place. Being away from the U.S., you tend to forget how simple things were, how to get from place to place, and that you can get almost anything delivered or visit and shop at your favorite stores easily.

As we know, everything has its advantages and disadvantages, no matter which country you live in. Let's get this straight; no place is *perfect*. The grass is not always greener on the other side. I've learned that the hard way several times. I am in my mid-30s and still trying to oversee the facade that others display; how great everything is on their social media accounts—reminding myself that everyone's lawns are the same shade of green or brown, depending on the day. Almost everyone on social media projects their highlight reel, not the real behind-the-scenes. I'm a victim of that too, but aren't we all? Living in a foreign country can be exotic, exhilarating, and rejuvenating, but you, other expats out there, all know that's not what our lives always seemed like. We go through so much turmoil, frustration, anxiety, and other emotions when adjusting to a new place, especially in a new country.

Each chapter in this book is about a specific topic that is emphasized or pointed out that others and I have noticed in our repatriation journey. But when I moved back to the U.S., I started to realize how these areas are ongoing issues, and it's nice to point these out and become more aware of the situations.

I will also share some pros of living back in the United States, of which there are many, and share a few tips that helped me readjust and how I found ways to save a bit of money. As you know, the United States lifestyle isn't the cheapest!

Those who have had the same experiences as I had, I hope you will be reading this book, nodding your head, and saying one or many of the following:

"Yes, I totally agree!"

"That's happened to me!"

"That's so true!"

"Why are we still in this same situation here? It's like living in the twilight zone!"

"How come we're still in the 1990s when it comes to necessary paperwork?"

"Why do we have so much cereal?"

"I can't find food that doesn't have added sugar in it!"

"Too many choices of this one brand!"

"Why is health insurance so expensive?"

I experienced this term called reverse culture shock when I readjusted. *Reverse culture shock*[1] is coming back to your home from your host country, and things are not the same or feel different once you get settled. It's a great feeling, as they say, the honeymoon phase; everything seems shiny, a great refresher, and all "hunky-dory." As the phases continue, the returnee realizes that friends and family have continued their lives, and no one wants to hear about your experiences overseas, well, maybe some of them. The returnee can become a bit overwhelmed, maybe more than a bit, especially in my case, due to the cultural differences of their home country. When readjusting to their new life, the returnee may feel out of sync, left out, or excluded from their culture.

Now, I have spent seven years overseas, and as I stated before, I will share with you a few of my experiences of living outside the United States and then mostly about returning to the United States. I left the States in my late 20s and returned back in my early 30s. This overseas experience has opened my eyes to new possibilities, a fresh taste palette of food,

---

[1] State.gov website, https://2009-2017.state.gov/m/fsi/tc/c56075.htm

and unique cultures! During this period overseas, there were new adventures, as well as, obstacles every day. Still, I would do it all over again, and everyone should have a chance to experience living (not just traveling) overseas. I have lived in China, Vietnam, Egypt, and, hopefully, more countries in the near future. I hope my journey living overseas hasn't ended, and this wanderlust bug will rejuvenate me.

If you have had the opportunity to live abroad, wasn't it a completely different experience than what you have faced back in your home country? What obstacles have you faced? If you moved back home already, would you move back overseas again?

When explaining to someone who has never left your home country, it's like speaking a foreign language to them. Trying to retell your experiences to those who haven't shared the same experience is hard, and getting them to understand where you came from is even more difficult. In America, acquiring the things you need is relatively easy. Sometimes, things here are archaic. For example, while living abroad, many services in other countries existed before the U.S. tagged on, such as grocery delivery and paying for items using just your phone. All my information and money was on my phone while living abroad. I rarely carried my wallet around with me.

Now, onto my latest moving experience from overseas, which some days I still have PTSD (post-traumatic stress disorder), and it's been two years since we moved back to the U.S.

Let's say the beginning of our 2021 moving journey didn't start on the right foot. I have had a job offer in another country since late autumn of 2020. I had all my paperwork ready to go until it was time to apply for a visa to enter that country, which I applied for around April 2021.

I had to wait for quite some time to see if my visa was going to be approved or not. It was June when my visa got denied with no explanation. The representatives at the visa office gave me a vague explanation why it was denied. I left that visa office in tears.

I was so angry and upset after all the prepping and paying people to handle the necessary documents preparing my cat to move with me. Then, most of all, I took my remaining sick days to run around Cairo to get my documents stamped and notarized. I wasted so much time and money on this move. During that time, my husband couldn't move with me due to the host country denying entry for dependents, so he had a plan B to move to another country in close proximity until the borders opened for him to enter, which still wasn't guaranteed at the time. Everything seemed hopeless, and I did not know when the pandemic would end. With all that, on top of the PCR (Polymerase Chain Reaction) testing, I couldn't handle any more stress. Time was not on my side at that point. I needed a plan B—a new job.

After hearing that my visa was denied, I had to talk to my new school about the next steps, whether to keep trying to apply again, work remotely until I get the visa, or cut ties with them. In some cases, if you cut ties or break a contract with a school, especially when using a recruitment agency, you could be blacklisted, develop a bad reputation towards other schools, and even owe money, depending on the agency you used. Unfortunately, this was my ultimate fear. I feared facing these consequences and was unsure what would happen. I prayed about it, hit the situation head-on, explained it to my recruitment agency, and spoke with my new school. My school and I most likely had to break the contract and part ways. But first, I needed to explain the situation to my recruitment agency. I was shaking while typing my email to them in hopes they would understand, especially with this pandemic.

After my agency got back to me, they completely understood and told me to keep them updated about my new school. Then I spoke with my new school about the next step of my limited choices. In the end, we did a peaceful release where no party was harmed or responsible due to the pandemic. I didn't have to owe that school or the recruitment agency any money. Thank goodness. It was time to move forward and quickly find a new job before the school year started. This was the beginning of July 2021. No job and to think that most school years start at the end of July, beginning of August. I was panicking at this point because jobs were limited.

Thankfully, I found some vacancies and went through a few rounds of interviews. It was down to a school in Germany and a school in Texas. I had to think long-term because I had to pick a school where the transition would be easier, and where my husband could come to the country since he's not a U.S. citizen. So, after discussing it, we picked the private school in Texas. We made the right choice, for many reasons.

I pray like crazy before any travels or moving, hoping to have smooth journeys. Prayers always worked for me, but there were plenty of times when I didn't have the best situations with flights, got sick, or other issues popped up. However, I always got from point A to point B in one piece, some way or another. The perks of traveling, there's always a risk and a chance of something awful happening. However, if you assume something wrong will happen, it most likely will happen.

I'm ready to tell you the full story of our return to the United States. So please sit back, get comfortable, have a glass of wine, and let's begin.

We left early in the morning on our last day in Egypt. It was mid-July 2021. We went in two cars. One of the drivers was our driver who took us around during most of our time in Egypt, and the other driver he hired to help us with this move. It was my husband, myself, two cats, and a few suitcases in one car, and in the other car were our remaining suitcases. We had a total number of nine suitcases (I would admit eight of them were most likely mine, while my husband had one small bag).

When we arrived at the international airport, around three and a half hours before departure, we had to get a massive cart for our suitcases, and we were officially ready to face this move head-on.

Our first hurdle was going through the first of the thousand scanners they make you go through as you trudge your way through the airport. It's a never-ending maze at this particular airport. They had several checkpoints, which makes it even more overwhelming because you seem that you're at the finish line, on the gangway before heading onto the airplane, but then, nope, you're facing another security guard to check your documents, suitcase, or, in this case, your PCR test.

Someone told us to get ready to take our cats out of the carriers to go through the first large scanner. I glared at the security guards and argued that getting our cats into the carrier was a hassle, let alone taking them out for a split second and trying to wrestle them back into the carrier. That was going to be a big, fat "No." After arguing and persuading the guards, they shooed us through with our cats inside their carriers—first hurdle done.

The next hurdle to overcome was checking in for our flight. Our fingers and toes crossed as we walked up to the check-in line. We had that fear in the back of our minds because anything could happen. We hoped to check in all our bags, ensure our cats were on our reservation, and that my husband could quickly leave the country to fly to America with ease.

We were the second ones to wait in line. There was a family of four ahead of us, who were already at the counter, which seemed by their looks and emotions they were having a rough start, too. They had four to five suitcases, all opened and spread out because it seemed they had to condense their items into only a few suitcases. Been there and done that. Piling additional suitcases into your already allotted checked bags is expensive. The husband stood there while the wife was scrambling to ensure things were not left behind, and having her kids help too. The husband and wife were arguing with each other, and I don't blame them because airline policies can be fickle and not clear about how many suitcases you can bring or let you know the exact price of each additional bag. I had researched and called the airline we flew from Egypt to the U.S. several times to ensure they understood that we had two cats coming on board, not as cargo, and bringing additional suitcases than the maximum checked bags that were included on our airline tickets. Sometimes, the language barrier and miscommunication are a headache when making airline reservations online because, on this airline, you have to do everything on the phone, especially when booking pets to fly with you. Then you have anxiety until you're about to fly, hoping they have the correct number of pets flying with you. And since COVID protocols were still in place, you must check if the PCR test is valid and negative before getting the green light to fly.

I hated PCR tests because getting a PCR test and calculating the time to get it done within the time window of flying and arriving at your final destination was stressful and gave you a massive migraine. You became a math whiz after calculating the hours to a T to ensure you entered the country within seventy-two hours after getting the nose swab test.

So, after the family of four checked in, which was about a solid forty-five minutes later, it was finally our turn. Everything so far was smooth; they had our reservations and our cats' reservations and even checked our PCR tests. I was more stressed about having the exact documents for the cats to fly. With just one mistake or the wrong paper, the airline can turn you away and not allow you or your pets on the flight. My anxiety has escalated since living overseas because of the tedious paperwork of getting the correct documentation, stamps, and exact wording done for your next country's destination. The lady at the counter just glanced at the veterinary papers, and that was it—all that stress and work up for nothing.

Then the counter lady said something that spiked our stress back up. My husband and I both booked a one-way ticket to the U.S. However, since my husband is Canadian and doesn't have a green card, the lady said he might not be allowed to fly to our final destination in Florida. We were shocked because Canadians can enter the U.S. with no issues, no visa, and can stay in the U.S. for up to six months. However, the lady perceived that my husband would have trouble and that he would have to book another ticket to Canada. So, my husband got out his credit card, ready to pay for this stupid additional plane ticket so we wouldn't face any issues when we arrived at JFK airport. Thankfully, the lady said, "Oh, no, you don't have to pay here, but maybe when you get to JFK, have a ticket booked to Canada just in case." Our hearts sank and rose within that two-minute conversation. I pulled out my phone and double-checked everything, and it didn't say anywhere that my husband didn't need a ticket to Canada as his final destination. So, we decided to wait and cross that bridge when we got there, especially on U.S. soil, because, at this point, it's much easier to book a flight there than to book from Egypt.

After that heart attack, we hauled and checked in all the suitcases, and thankfully, my husband could take some of mine to add to his ticket to decrease the price than for me to put the eight or so suitcases on just my ticket. Once we had our tickets, it didn't matter in the end how much we spent on a one-way trip, nine suitcases, and two cats. We just wanted to leave. We spent about $1400 per person, including the cat fee and the extra baggage. I grabbed our airline tickets with a massive sigh of relief. But my husband was still apprehensive of the next hurdle—getting our cats out of their travel bags through the next checkpoint.

Next, we headed to the security checkpoint where we would most likely have to take our cats out of the carriers. The checkpoint guy rechecked our PCR test papers. Then they checked our paper-printed itinerary (yes, they still do the old-school way of printing the confirmation email of your ticket, and using an electronic copy on your phone wasn't acceptable at that point), and they made us go to separate scanners, which didn't make sense since we booked our tickets together. We both took off our shoes and any items to put through the conveyor belt, along with our carry-on suitcases and personal items.

I told the security guard I needed to take my cat out of his carrier because they told us the cat or dog had to go through the scanner where the suitcases go! It wasn't happening. I told my husband to give them a hard no if they try to argue. Who puts animals through an X-ray scanner with the luggage? I prayed my cat wouldn't run off once I opened his carrier because he was petrified of the noise and crowds. Then, the pressure is on to hurry through the scanner, with the other guests who were rushing to get through the line. This situation didn't help my stress, and my cat could sense my anxiety, which didn't help him stay calm either. I was prepared for the cat claws today because I wore my thick jean jacket for this special occasion. Once I took my cat out of the carrier, he grasped onto me while I held him with one hand and cradled him while holding his harness. The security guy waved me to come through, and everything was good. I put my cat back into his carrier.

I was now ahead of my husband at the security line. He was still a ways back from having his turn to go through the scanner with his cat. Once I got my carry-on and put on my shoes, I had to go through a walkway, so it was hard to see where my husband was in the line. I found a spot where I could vaguely see him; but I knew his turn was coming up. I saw him physically put his carry-on through the X-ray scanner while holding onto his cat. But it took a while because the security guards were speaking to him and not letting him through. That wasn't a good sign. I saw him holding his cat but not moving much forward. The next second, he wasn't there anymore, and I was, "What the heck?" Panic mode started to set in. I was pacing back and forth while carrying my cat on my shoulder hoping to see my husband turn the corner.

It was about ten minutes later, and we were about to board soon; I was getting quite nervous. What happens if they don't let my husband through? It's either all of us on this flight or not. When it felt like a century later, he came out of the line with his cat in the carrier on his shoulder, in the same direction I did a while ago. His facial expression said it all. He looked so stressed, and he took a deep breath and said, "I thought I was going to get arrested."

"What happened?" It was moments before boarding would start.

He said, "Make sure to take out your batteries before packing your carry-on."

"Batteries?"

"They thought I was creating some bomb with my lithium batteries, and I nearly argued and reassured them it was a simple mistake and the batteries were from my game controller. They even brought an additional military police officer with an AK-47 to threaten that I would go to prison if I didn't tell them the truth."

"What the actual–"

"Then they argued with me that my cat has to go through the x-ray scanner or she won't be able to board. And I kept telling them no and that it could harm the cat. So, they told me to go to this nearby room so I could take her out of the carrier, and they could check her carrier to see if there was anything suspicious. My poor cat clung to me, terrified. And worst of all, they rechecked my carry-on suitcase several more times after it went through the x-ray scanner."

We both said, "We can't wait to leave here."

I just rolled my eyes and reassured my husband that everything was okay and we were heading to the States now. The second we said this, they called us to board the plane, just in the nick of time. We grabbed all our items, cats, and PCR tests because they would do the thousandth check of the PCR document before we got onto the plane. We raced towards the front because they let anyone through after they called the priority and gold members. There are no "zones" when boarding flights in Egypt; it's like a herd of elephants cramming through a tiny gate door. We walked down a ramp, and there was yet another security checkpoint, where they checked our passports and PCR tests. Then finally, we were through. We had our tickets in our hands and found our seats. Our cats were, at this point, terrified, and it was the first time for both of our cats to fly in the cabin with us. My cat has flown in cargo before, and I won't do that again. He will be by my side on the plane beside me, not beneath me.

I never felt so much joy when we started taxiing on the runway. Our cats were at our feet, and we petted them to help calm them down and reassure them that everything was okay. The plane did take off on time and finally ascended into the air. We looked out the window and said, "Good riddance!" We may have recalled saying a few curse words as we viewed Cairo from above.

I'm not bashing the people of Egypt because the people I've met have been lovely. But how some things were organized there could have been handled better. When others who lived in Egypt had a different experience than us and thought, why wouldn't you love Egypt? It has so much to offer. Not us. We had more bad experiences than good. My husband and I both agreed we would likely never go back. Our cat, Hattie, was one of the best souvenirs we brought from Egypt.

The flight from Egypt to New York felt like it took no time at all. It was a solid twelve hours of flying. The flight was smooth, the cats were good, we watched a few movies and ate an edible meal. Once we arrived in New York around 6:30 p.m., we had all our papers ready when we got into the immigration line. My husband had his Nexus card, which means he could skip the long immigration lines and go through the Global Entry line instead. However, since we didn't want to get separated, we decided to go through the immigration line together. However, our two cats were the showstoppers because everyone in the immigration line kept asking us their names and backstories and trying to sweet talk to them.

The line seemed to shorten quickly, and soon, it was our turn to talk to the immigration officer. They did the protocol of asking what we were here for (more for my husband than for me) and showed our cats' paperwork. But then they wanted us to go to another location to give our cats the official clearance to the U.S. The immigration officer checked our PCR tests and passports, and that was it. He led us to where we needed to go next for our cats' document checkpoint. We had to grab all our suitcases along the way since we had booked another ticket from New York to Tampa. We had a final destination flight to Tampa. Still, for the second leg of our flight, we couldn't add our cats to our reservation, and getting a hold of this specific airline was nearly impossible, so we just canceled the second leg after finding out we couldn't get our cats on that second reservation. We had to book a flight from JFK to Tampa with another airline. Thankfully, talking to this airline was straightforward and didn't have to be on hold for several hours. Dealing with them was a breeze and verifying that our cats were on our ticket reservation was a piece of cake. Also, adding our extra baggage was simple, unlike the other airline we were supposed to fly on for the second leg of our flight to Tampa.

After gathering our luggage, we went to the desk, where they would check our cats' paperwork. It took a few minutes since no one was there, and when an officer arrived, he just glanced at our cat carriers, looked at the paperwork, and cleared us. Bringing cats into the States was easier than I thought. I stressed out our veterinarian from Egypt, asking him and double-checking that our cats' paperwork was not going to be problematic, but he reassured me that bringing cats into the States was easy and that we shouldn't experience any issues. And he was right. I learned to take people's word for it, especially if they're experts in those areas.

Since we got our luggage from the Egypt flight, we had to check back in again. Thankfully the check-in counters were close by and we made it in the line just before the crowds started showing up.

Then, I saw the flight assistants directing the customers, not-so-nicely, by telling them to get in line to check their bags. One flight assistant said, "I can't believe people can't read." I stared at her in shock, hearing a professional say this aloud. The check-in counter location was in this tiny, cramped place with limited room for the luggage carts, and there needed to be a direct sign of where to stand honestly. Some of the things I've heard from airline workers shocked me, especially when they talk out loud, thinking no one can understand or hear them. It isn't polite. It can be annoying when people need to follow directions, but people must remember that flying long distances wears you down, and you may be too tired to think. I feel ashamed when I see tourists coming to America treated this way.

Next, we encountered a rude lady behind us who thought it was okay for her child to kick our suitcases and cat carriers since they were right on our tails in the line. I kindly told her to have her child stop kicking our cats, which fumed me because our cats were already stressed out. The lady flipped out and yelled at me. Funny thing, she turns to her friend and starts speaking in French. I know a bit of French but can't understand everything, but I knew some words she was saying, and they weren't kind. I laughed, turned around, and told my husband she was bad-mouthing us in French. Funny enough, my husband speaks French since that is his first language. He turns around and tells her in French, "We had a long flight as well, and please ask your child to stop kicking our cats while they are in their carriers."

Of course, the lady didn't respond well and gave me a dirty look, and my husband just turned back around to ignore her. We were back in the U.S.; if you start a battle with someone, you know you will show up on a TikTok video. So, we decided to ignore the woman and press on, hoping this line would shorten.

Once we checked in our gazillion bags, each bag ended up at least 23 kg (50 pounds). I had to pay another reservation fee for both of our cats and finally, we were good to go.

After all this chaos, we were starving. We packed a few snacks but needed more until we reached Florida. Our cats were also thirsty; unfortunately, there wasn't a pet relief area nearby in the terminal. I tried to give water and some food to both our cats during our trip, but they didn't want either of the options. I also felt bad because they probably needed to use a litter box. Thankfully, we packed some pee pads in their carriers and brought spares, just in case.

In the airport, there were limited options for food places, especially during the pandemic. Most places were still closed. We found this restaurant where they seemed fine when we brought in our cats. The menu had some limited options, nothing too appetizing or appealing, but something was better than nothing. We ordered and asked the waitress for small cups of water to give to our cats. Chandler licked most of his water while Hattie was having none of it. I took some and dabbed her mouth with water so she could lick some, to avoid dehydration. Let's say she's a stubborn traveling companion. We got our food and ate it so fast because we had to make our next flight. We paid the bill and waited for our change. However, the waitress never returned our change.

Once we saw her, we asked for our change back, and she said, "Oh, I kept it because it was my tip."

I looked at my husband and thought, isn't it always required to return leftover change to a customer, no matter how much you have left? Has something changed since I left the States years ago? We told her we would like to get our change back and then give her a tip. She flipped out and caused this huge scene in front of the other guests at the restaurant. I was appalled by her behavior.

She said, "I even gave your cats water!"

I replied, "Yes, but we should still get our change back, and then we will tip." We always tipped, but today, with her nasty behavior, she didn't deserve a tip. I know I will get karma for this, but I didn't feel bad when the service was crap, especially with her erratic behavior.

Before you judge now, I was in the food industry years ago. I get it. Tipping helps you get by because the hourly wages are a joke. However, from my waitressing experience, I always put the customers first and treated them respectfully, whether customers were friendly or rude. Sometimes, I didn't get a tip, but I would never have flipped out on the customers like this waitress did. We got our change back and still ended up giving her a small tip, even after her unpleasant behavior and tone. We just kept our mouths shut and didn't argue back at her, especially who knows who would record you and put you on social media. Keeping quiet was the wisest decision. After ignoring the screaming waitress, we gathered our items and cats and strolled out of the restaurant.

We needed to head to our gate when we exited the restaurant. Once we arrived, we sat down for a few minutes before they started to call for boarding. On this last leg, we each bought a first-class ticket because we got an extra bag allowance and easier to carry our cats, and two, we got to board first. Even though the tickets were pricey, I just wanted our last flight to be as smooth as possible.

Thankfully, we got on board, and at this point, I knew our cats were exhausted and annoyed and ready to be out of their carriers. This flight was thankfully around three hours, and soon, we would be in Florida. Once we boarded, Hattie officially had her anxiety attack. She started to foam from her mouth and bawled loudly. I'm sure others could hear our screeching cat from the front of the plane. I began to freak out because I didn't know why she was doing this, and I gathered as many tissues and napkins as possible to wipe away the foam from her mouth. Of course, my husband put the carrier on his lap until take-off to ensure she was okay. I quickly texted my vet back in Egypt about the situation, and he said it was just travel anxiety. So, having a peaceful last leg of the flight didn't happen. Hattie did this for most of the flight, then calmed down right before we landed. We didn't get our money's worth on first-class tickets.

After what seemed an eternity to us, we finally arrived in Tampa. There is no better feeling than seeing a familiar face greeting you at the airport—my mom. She picked us up and was mentally ready to pack our million suitcases into her car. My mom was a rockstar in figuring out how to play Tetris with our suitcases. She even prepared herself using her own suitcases by figuring out how to organize them so our bags would all fit before our arrival. The cats were good, and we still had another hour and a half drive to my parents' house. After calculating the hours spent in the airport, in the air, and driving, it was a total of twenty-three hours. It's way too long, especially with our cats.

My mom had litter boxes prepped for our cats and would stay in a separate room because she didn't want her cats to get mad and pee everywhere. The second we arrived at my parents' house, I took our cats straight to their litter boxes and gave them some fresh water and the cat food we gave them in Egypt. I know our cats were excited to finally relieve themselves, eat, run, and hide for the remainder of the evening. I was just happy everyone made it to Florida.

We had a few busy, stressful weeks ahead of us because I was supposed to start my new job in Houston, and we didn't have our place yet. We still had a long way to go before I had to move again and start my new job within thirteen days.

Chapter 2

What's That Noise?

"I remember going to Walmart after returning home for the summer. I had a superpower where, all of a sudden, I could understand everyone's conversation. It was like a million voices talking at once. I became so overwhelmed to the point I had to leave the store. It was too much for me to handle."

-Lisa, who lived abroad for eight years.

One of the perks of living back home is understanding the language, where almost everyone speaks the same language. When living overseas, you don't understand the spoken language, so it's "easier" to let it go through one ear and out the other or block it out completely. However, I loved being overseas and listening to several languages, which pushed me to learn many words, phrases, and conversation starters to get by at the time. It's the downfall of growing up in the U.S., where speaking a second language is unnecessary. Back in school, you may have electives where you can choose Latin (which I don't understand why you are learning a language that no one speaks anymore, or at least I am aware of), French, or even Spanish classes in high school. Still, we all know we didn't learn much during those school years. I took Spanish for two years and all I learned was how to say a poem about a dog in Spanish. I wish our school systems pushed us to pursue learning a second language and highlight the importance of speaking another language than just English.

I received shocking responses when I told people from back home that I taught overseas. The first question was, "That means you, like, do you just teach English to these kids?" "How do you communicate if you don't understand one another?"

On the inside, I was giggling because they thought I had become fluent in all the languages I had to speak while living in these countries. I don't blame others for asking those questions; they're legitimate. They don't know because they haven't experienced this. If they never have the experience, why would I expect them to know about this? But in a friendly tone, I reply, "No, I teach all core subjects that an elementary teacher would teach here in the States, such as Language Arts, Math, Science, and Social Studies." It was a repeated script for sure when talking to others back home.

"So, that means you can speak their language fluently?" If I had a hundred dollars each time someone asked me this question; I would've been swimming in money.

"No, not necessarily. I have wonderful teacher assistants and staff who help and translate for us when needed. Plus, speaking fluent Mandarin, Vietnamese, and Arabic is impossible unless I take classes full-time."

Believe it or not, most students can speak and comprehend English in many schools, especially internationally. It's unbelievable, yet mind-blowing that many students speak at least three languages. How sad is it when I encounter these families and other people I meet worldwide to tell them I only speak one language? Several students in the past had snickered at me while trying to talk with the correct tones in Mandarin and Vietnamese. The tones were so much harder for me in Vietnamese; I just gave up because it was hard to repeat anything. I chose to sit back and listen to the Vietnamese communicate with each other. Their language is so soothing that I dream off in a fantasy land, back to what I was saying about the students laughing at you for trying to say a word in their language, when in fact, your tone makes the word sound and mean something completely different if not stated correctly. In the end, they will value the fact that you are trying to learn their language. There's no greater reward than that. You will be surprised how much you can pick up from the students. They are the best teachers.

Previously when I came back to the U.S. for a trip, it was actually to get married; I was overwhelmed by all the conversations I could hear and understand all of them at once. Usually, I need to remember that most people speak English. It was overstimulating, for sure, especially on a Vegas bus! Your eyes and ears go in all directions listening to everyone's conversations when you don't do it on purpose! Some of the conversations you wish you could ignore due to being inappropriate. It was challenging to tune out.

Learning the language of the country we live in, we were encouraged to learn some phrases while living in a specific country to help us get from place to place. Also, Google Translate was my saving grace, which sometimes was inconsistent because of the confused looks when asking questions on that app. Other apps helped me as well, especially with translating Mandarin. Trying to communicate with those who didn't speak English was a daily challenge overseas. It was one of the top frustrations as an expat, especially when documentation was needed.

I don't know if others can relate, but watching body language and hand gestures (not the middle finger) helped me understand what someone was talking about when there was a language barrier. Also, learning the Chinese numbers was fun, especially when showing how many quantities of food you needed at the wet market (a place to buy meat, fish, and produce).

Houston is a vast melting pot of culture all around, and I love Houston for that, which is one of the main reasons I like living here. I can visit many parts of the city and see diversity everywhere. I love that if I miss any Asian food, I can go to an Asian town, find a good bowl of Pho, although quite expensive, and reminisce about my times in Asia. I can also sip on some good Tsingtao beer. The best part of living in Houston is that my extracurricular activities involve getting my hair touched up, my nails done, and taking dance classes, and where I go, it makes me think I'm in a different country at times. I love talking to the people there, and we will sit and chat about all the great times in Asia. It's fantastic when your hairstylist has lived in the same city as you did in Vietnam, and you can talk for hours about the restaurants, beaches, and events in Saigon.

I miss the connections with people who had similar experiences, and they understand and know what you're talking about. It's a great feeling. It's pretty soothing to sit and listen to the Vietnamese and Chinese have conversations together, and you're like, "Yep, I remember that phrase and word, vaguely, but it's coming back or quickly picks up when your ballet teacher who is Chinese, tell you what you're doing wrong in Chinese." Languages are so fascinating. I can't say it enough. In all, I probably say, "I miss living overseas." daily. I would make it back overseas someday. To the expats who lived in a country for some time and then moved back to the U.S., you know when you have a piece of your heart that belongs to that host country. It's your second or even your first home, making the U.S. your second.

You must see this movie if you have yet to see *The 355* and miss the international lifestyle and elements. They hopped, skipped, and jumped to different cities worldwide, and you hear many languages in just one scene, and it's incredible! The movie didn't receive the best reviews, but if you miss that overseas experience, watch it still. Also, the film focuses on women and how they rock at their jobs and missions. My husband and I favor more movies that involve the international experience and seeing the different cities and countries, either reminiscing about these places or wishing one day to go there.

However, being back home in your home country has been a world-changer, and almost everyone speaks your mother tongue. It's so convenient when you can understand everything again and not have to pick up my Google Translate on my phone. The overwhelming feeling of hearing everyone talking in English has dwindled after living here during the first few months, and I have adjusted to background noise. Occasionally, I hear someone speaking in Chinese, Vietnamese, French, and Arabic. I try to slip in Chinese, Vietnamese, and French words, but my tones are so off they give me quizzical looks. I still love hearing other languages, and I want to keep the French I've learned over the last few years because there's no point in using it in a country where I don't need it to get around. However, it may push me to keep learning French because I am still determined to keep traveling and never know when I will bump into someone who only speaks French.

To strengthen my French, I was determined to take some tutoring classes and listen to some podcasts on my way to work. If I want to escape, I listen to various podcasts in several languages. I even started learning some Spanish too. I traveled to Central and South America the last few summers, inspiring me to learn and speak Spanish.

Chapter 3

Driving!

"Cars seem aggressively enormous, don't they? Oh, wait, most U.S. cities are not pedestrian-friendly, and I'm in the land of the agricultural biotechnology corporations. Who needs public transportation in the land of the individualist? Not to worry, restaurants do serve massive portions of food, though. That's a win! Why can't I walk, ride my bike, take a bus or train to most places without getting run over or shanked?!"

-Eric, who lived abroad for ten years.

What can I say? Driving in the United States is insane! Completely insane and barbaric by all means. I've never seen so much passive-aggressive driving. The drivers need to be more impatient and more careful. They don't believe in yellow lights. They call them pink lights here. You don't slow down at a yellow light but speed up before the light turns red. If you're new to driving in Texas, you learn to look behind you if you come up to a yellow light. It depends on the timing because the lights from yellow to red change slowly or fast.

I love it when people speed and tailgate you and then pass you (when you're not in a passing lane), and then they cut you off. I always say what is the rush? Do you need to make it to your happy hour to get that 2-for-1 deal, or do you need to get to your dry cleaning place before the store closes? The best one I heard from someone was, "He must have diarrhea; that's why he's in a race to the nearest toilet."

After living in Houston, pickup trucks, especially the gigantic ones, make me nervous. They run on your behind by tailgating you to speed up, which you obviously can't because you have a slower driver ahead of you. I've learned to always keep at least a car distance from the person in front of me, just in case of the possibility of getting rear-ended. The monster trucks will then almost clip you as they zoom past you and speed up on the highway, and I think you just sucked more gas out of your car by hitting the accelerator.

Also, has anyone ever heard of a turn signal when switching lanes or turning at a freaking light?

I also asked myself, "Why do people not turn their headlights on at dusk or dawn?" I am at the point where I leave my headlights on "automatic" so they are turned on for other drivers to see me. Some still drive without turning on their headlights, driving down the highway, and even on off-roads. You can barely see them as they go past you.

Learning how to drive again is like riding a bicycle. It takes time, but it's easy once you get the hang of it. But driving a moving truck, no. I hated driving one of those when moving across several states, and having no rear-view mirror threw me off tremendously. Thankfully, my husband drove the majority of the trip. I couldn't tell you how often we thought the brakes needed to be stronger when stopping that moving truck, and you had to slow down sooner than expected. Also, we drove through the night with all our belongings, two cats, and maybe four hours of sleep. That was the dumbest decision we probably made in a while, and we have made some pretty bad choices. But driving straight through for almost twenty hours with limited sleep was not such a smart decision. We must have some guardian angel protecting us because we drove like zombies and didn't have our full attention on the road. We guzzled down fifteen cups of coffee to get us from Florida to Texas. Thankfully, we made it all in one piece, moved our stuff into our new apartment, and even started my new job the next day.

I drove like a slow poke for the first few weeks when I arrived back home, and once I got a car, I was even more careful because many drivers were lunatics and terrified me while I was behind the wheel. I thought there were crazy drivers overseas, but it's even worse here! You have a mix of drivers here; some are from out of state.

Once I started driving here, my defensive driving eventually took over. I think I ask myself aloud, "How did this person get their driver's license?" because of all the unbelievable stunts they pull while driving, from cutting people off to seeing people get out of their cars after they lose their tempers from other drivers. Then you have to worry about not pissing people off because who knows if people carry certain items.

This rule applies to any driver on a highway; always keep an eye on the car or vehicle in front of you at all times. The drivers coming up on your sides would be your next glance. I worry less about the drivers surrounding me than those in front of me, especially if they come to a complete stop.

I also noticed that and must see if using your cellular phone while driving is legal or illegal. We must make necessary calls, but it's wise to refrain from using your phone, especially texting, while driving.

Another thing that was a shock is wearing seatbelts again here. Don't get me wrong; I tried to wear seatbelts overseas, whether in someone else's car or taking an Uber. Believe it or not, many cars didn't have seatbelts in the backseats, which was alarming, but what could I do? I said a prayer or two when those instances happened because there were so many car accidents daily where I lived and visited overseas.

I vividly remember when I came home to visit my family in the U.S., and I decided to rent a car during my stay. The best thing about coming back home to see it is that you can talk to almost anyone about your adventures overseas, and most of the time, people are intrigued and will ask all sorts of questions. The attendant at the car rental place talked with me, and I told the attendant I lived in Egypt. His next question, and I kid you not, was, "So, do you ride a camel to work?" I just grinned and was waiting for this opportunity to arise where I could have some fun and, you know, be a smart aleck but mean no harm.

I replied, "Oh yeah! The school I work for provides us with transportation, and they gave me a camel to get to and from work each day."

"What! No way!" said the attendant.

"Yep! I had to ensure I gave myself enough time to work on time because camels are quite slow during the trek. Traffic can be horrible, so I must leave at least two hours early to get to work on time."

I finally grinned and said to him that I was only joking.

In Vietnam, we got around by motorcycles or taxis. Riding on motorcycles was one of my favorite memories of living in Vietnam. The streets in Vietnam were always filled with motorbikes. Families would squeeze and fit onto one motorbike from four to five people! How is that possible? Yes, it was also dangerous riding on motorbikes, and I know a few people who got into accidents and came out with severe injuries. Taking an Uber or a Grab bike was more accessible than taking a car or taxi within the city. In Egypt, I rode a bus to and from work provided by the school, and most days, I was nauseous due to the twists, turns, and bumps on the unpaved roads. So, every day to me was a risk when using transportation overseas.

I've seen some crazy overseas driving and things I would see there, but less often in the States. For example, I saw a taxi full of oranges, all in the backseat of a taxi in Egypt. I did a double-take and pinched myself, making sure what I saw was real. In countries, drivers transport random items on the highway that are stacked mountains high and can magically not fly off while driving at excessive speeds. On other days, there were mountains high of chicken crates to even styrofoam pieces on the back of a small truck, strapped down while zooming on the highways, and surprisingly, nothing would have flown off.

If you have a car, I suggest buying a dash cam. Buying one was the best advice if you're driving a lot, especially in the States. Some drivers have become more reckless these days. Many might even blame you for an accident that was entirely their fault. It's also nice to see who dings up your nicely parked car in the parking lot because more people are prone to doing that. Banging up the side of your car and not even leaving a sorry note about scratching your car shows how inconsiderate people can be. It's already expensive with car maintenance, let alone car insurance, and the hassle of calling your insurance company to file a claim, on top of being charged outrageous prices to get your car fixed. I bought a front and rear dash cam and felt more peace of mind. Incredibly, the camera can still record while the vehicle is parked. A sensor will go off if there are any motions or movements near your parked vehicle.

When stopping at a red light, I love it when someone is so close to my tail, and I say to myself, *drive a little closer because if you rear-end me, I've got you on candid camera!*

There are so many massive pickup trucks in Texas, especially in Houston. Then you have the minority of truck drivers who speed like demons on the highway. A truck driver was cutting corners while his American flag was waving. I was waiting to turn right, and a car was in front of me, but this trucker needed to go between us. I couldn't move at all on the tight-fitted highway. This truck driver dared to honk and yell out his window to the car in front of me to pull forward (which the driver had limited space to do) for no reason. It's like, "Chill, dude, you're only going to a store, not to meet a celebrity." The lack of common courtesy with aggressive driving and people losing their patience still flusters me.

Chapter 4

Foods Galore!

"Abroad, I had gotten in the habit of meeting friends or my husband for drinks, coffee, or a snack after work. It was a common concept in Greece, and one I quickly adapted to. Once work was done, it was done, and it was time to relax. Afternoons and evenings were meant to go by slowly and be a time to relax and connect with others. Meeting up after work could last nearly two hours and no one rushed. Once I moved back to the U.S., everyone had a long to-do list once work was done. Everyone seemed to be rushing around and never stayed long at a restaurant or coffee shop to just relax. I rarely saw friends after work because of this, and I could never understand why it seemed everyone here seemed to always be rushing."

-TD, who lived abroad for eight years.

Buying food in other countries can be a hit or miss. Sometimes certain food items will be in stock, while other times, you won't see them again for another couple of months. There are pros and cons of getting groceries overseas. Grocery delivery has been around for a while overseas. Who doesn't love all your groceries delivered right to your front doorstep? I also didn't have to pay an arm and a leg for the total amount, including the tip, when getting groceries delivered overseas. I enjoy going to the grocery store, buying the items, and having the staff deliver the items later instead of carrying the groceries back home. I have yet to order online and do curbside pickup here in the U.S. I prefer to pick out my produce since I am picky now with my fruit and vegetables. I know shoppers here prefer to order groceries online and do curbside pickup, but I still like to go inside the store and pick out the items I want.

Sometimes, grocery shopping can be frustrating overseas. You may have to shop around not one, but three different shops to find your grocery list items. For example, I may find some pasta noodles at this store, but then I need help finding the specific herbs I need at the same place. I would have to take another ride to another grocery store to see if they have those particular herbs in stock. My husband and I would have about three different grocery store apps and spend a good chunk of time navigating through all the apps and adding all the items we need to the cart. Hopefully, the items we put into the online cart would say they are in stock and maybe show up at your door within an hour. We checked our receipts religiously because sometimes we had missing items or the items were out of stock. We started ordering our groceries online in the last two years because, one, the pandemic, and two, the heat was becoming too brutal to go out and haul all these groceries in one go. Plus, I wanted to save money on transportation.

Arriving back in the U.S., you can take a nice grocery trip to Kroger, Walmart, or even an H-E-B (stores in Texas) and get all you usually need in one trip. It wasn't the fact I could get all my groceries at one location, but it was being completely overwhelmed by the vast amount of choices you have up and down the aisles of food. A friend mentioned this was one of the first struggles to experience when moving back home—too many choices of food brands. I didn't know a company could create carrot cake Oreos (I love carrot cake but not as in Oreos) or Frosted Confetti Cupcake Pop-Tarts. Who would even think to try those flavors? What happened to the original Oreos (double stuffed Oreos are better) or strawberry Pop-tarts?

At first, I was like a kid in a candy store, full of excitement when I could buy every item on my grocery list at one stop. I was ecstatic to purchase some things because I hadn't seen that specific item in years. Only on my visit trips back home would I spoil myself, have these food items, and take the stock load back to my host country until my next visit back home.

Another shocking thing I and others have experienced is this: There is sugar in everything. I mean *everything*. It's disgusting. When I need to buy specific items for my meals, whether canned, jar, or packaged, I first glance at the ingredients; there's sugar and even added sugar! I can't escape it. I remember trying to find some dried fruit, not processed or with added sugar, and finding them was a definite challenge here. I eventually did, but I paid a lot of money for it. There is at least some kind of fructose or sucrose ingredient in any of those food items. Watching so many documentaries on the sugar content in foods is appalling, and sadly, we are addicted to sugar, which I still am, if I am frank. Cutting out sugar here is more challenging now than it was living abroad.

As I am walking around a store, it's depressing that my first instinct is to look at the nutrition facts label. It's either the high amounts of sugar or sodium that make up the taste of these processed or packaged items. I constantly examine the labels and ingredients when I go grocery shopping. When you realize the downright toxic ingredients to your body are still "approved," you can buy them off shelves. Anything that has aspartame, corn syrup, mimic sugars, and hydrogenated oils in it, I try to avoid them altogether. One particular example that I used to buy years ago was Coffee Mate. I used that stuff, powder or liquid, daily in my coffee, including three to four Splenda packets. I am surprised my body didn't shut down and went into a coma. I also drank Mountain Dew every afternoon when I started my teaching career. What the heck was I thinking? I call those cancers in a can. We could save our health if we become more aware of the nasty, toxic ingredients in many of these packaged items. One definite lesson I have learned over the years, and I can't believe it took me thirty years to figure this out, is that whatever you put into your body affects you and your outward appearance. As someone would say, health is wealth.

Being addicted to sugar is hard, especially when you're tempted to eat all the sweets in the bakery section in a grocery store or the delicious cookies in the teachers' lounge. Also, I get that brain fog from eating poorly. It's hard to even think of words you want to use in a conversation without saying, "I can't think of the word I'm trying to use, or it's on the tip of my tongue."

I have steered away from many fast-food chains, except for an occasional Chick-fil-a. You can't turn down mouth-watering waffle fries and those heavenly chicken nuggets. In addition, they do have the best seasonal peppermint chip milkshakes, even though there are harmful chemicals in the shakes! In most of the commercials or billboards I've seen, the fast food chain's items don't look quite delicious and give me heartburn when looking at them. I've learned from being back home that cooking at home is cheaper, and you know what you put into your meals. Plus, many fast food restaurants taste and look about the same. My husband and I will have an occasional fast food run, but we usually ask ourselves, "Why did we get this?" since we get a stomach ache immediately afterward. Plus, spending an average of twenty dollars for two people is too much for the amount you receive and then you're hungry a few hours later.

Believe it or not, there were McDonald's, Popeyes, and Burger King in all parts of the world. At the beginning of our Egypt journey, we got hooked on the french fries and chocolate fudge sundaes, which we had about three times a week! You would have thought we were pregnant, but no, it was the utter stress of transiting to Egypt. The funny thing is, I rarely ate McDonald's when living in the States, but when living overseas, you crave something that makes you think of home for some odd reason. Long story short, we gained significant weight from eating all those sundaes. Let's say we cut out McDonald's entirely and can't pass by a chain of them without gagging.

I want to mention portion sizes here in the U.S. I realized how significant the portions were when I came back to visit. The portion sizes are too plentiful and two people can share easily. The free, unlimited refills are obsolete overseas, but it's quite common here. Another shock that I faced was the sizes of drinks you ordered at fast food chains and restaurants. A small size is like a size medium or even large when ordering from a food place in another country. I ordered a small ice cream cone and it looked like a large size. I could barely finish it without getting sick.

When eating out in a restaurant here, my eyes are bigger than my stomach, so I order a few sides with an entree. It's a big mistake each time because I have loads of leftovers for days. I read that in other cultures, many people eat their meals at restaurants and do not take any leftovers home, but I still took them home when I lived in Asia and Africa.

But, the upside of returning to the U.S. is that I can get all my groceries and food fixings in one area. Yes, I still shop at local stores, but when I have an extensive grocery list, I go to a local or a popular chain grocery store. I finally learned to use my fuel points as a customer and fill up my tank much cheaper than at other chain gas stations. I realize how much I miss a car when I want to shop for groceries alone, not worrying about others delivering my items and possibly having the wrong set of objects, missing items, or even damaged ones sent to my front door.

I have also noticed that Americans will say that Asian food is delicious when they go to a Japanese steakhouse or a Chinese restaurant. Sadly, those certain style restaurants are not entirely "authentic." I realized what authentic Asian food tasted like in their countries while living or visiting there. Once you taste authentic food within that country, food seems to become more bland when moving back to the U.S. Don't get me wrong; I have found some places here that are pretty close to the taste of that cuisine, but you can still tell it has the American touch.

After educating myself on being careful of what I'm putting into my body, I have had experiences when ordering food where all the colors, including the side items, are the same. I am guilty of this when I have made Thanksgiving dinners, where many items are the same color. Corn, turkey, mashed potatoes, macaroni and cheese, and rolls, for example. They all taste delicious, but where are the different colors of vegetables on the platter? And not to mention the amount of starch and carbs on that plate. No wonder I went into a food coma after every Thanksgiving meal. My new habit, whether ordering food at a restaurant or cooking my meals, is to order or cook each food item in a different color. I also tried to add two different colored vegetable sides. Every day at work, I aim to eat a rainbow color of vegetables and fruits, which can be challenging, too, but it's a good habit to start.

After hearing and trying recommendations of food places from people, some businesses are good, while others could be better. If I had a dollar each time someone said I needed to try this XYZ place because it has the best XYZ, I would have a lump sum of cash in front of me. In the recommended places we try, the taste of the food usually could be better. Plus, you get recommendations from people who have never left the U.S. and may not know what authentic cuisine tastes like. Now, I will give the U.S. this; they can specialize in a good hamburger, chicken fried steak, and sub sandwiches. A good sub brings back childhood memories in Pennsylvania, which we call hoagies there! Also, if you want a specific order for your burger, you can get it easily customizable. Unlike overseas, ordering customized meals is rare, in my experience.

Food quality in restaurants, especially chain restaurants, has deteriorated over the last few years. It's not that good anymore, and I won't say which chain restaurants have lost their touch and a decent taste of food, but it seems to be a generic consensus from my taste buds. When I moved back, I thought I would attend these restaurants occasionally. I wanted to take my husband to some of these places, which we did, and we just looked at each other in disappointment. We have found a few decent restaurants in Houston and will go to them for special occasions.

While living in China and Vietnam, trying new foods was a significant adjustment. In the meantime, during your new move transition, you seek out familiar foods from your home country. My hook for a while was Kraft macaroni and cheese and Pop-Tarts. Both unhealthy for me, but they were familiar and felt a piece of home was with me. I became so hooked on Pop-tarts that I had my parents ship me boxes occasionally (along with other things I couldn't get in China) until some shops in China provided Pop-tarts at Western grocery stores. It's like Christmas when you see your favorite brands in those stores because you can't always find them. Once you see your item, you better get your supply while it lasts because you never know when you will see this item again.

Chapter 5

Geography

"That's the other tricky thing about moving away from the U.S. and then coming back. There are not many other first-world countries more dangerous and full of guns than ours, so coming from living in Asia, where we never once questioned our safety for six years, was a tough pill to swallow and a sacrifice we knew we were making. Suddenly, I felt worried about doing the simplest activities, like getting groceries after sunset or teaching my students at school. Having to practice with my second graders on how to do "intruder drills" was both scary and sad at the same time. Knowing the kindergarteners down the hall were also silently huddled in the corner of their classroom with the lights off while pretending boogie men jiggled the doors to the classroom to make sure they were locked was sad. That took some re-getting to get used to, for sure.

Coming from open classrooms with giant windows taking up entire walls in both Vietnam and Thailand, with doors that I'm not even sure had locks on them, to my new classroom in a trailer that was required to be locked at all times, that we weren't even allowed to have propped open when it was a beauty day out, that had four tiny windows that weren't allowed to be opened, was sad."

-Emily, who lived abroad for six and a half years.

Geography was my absolute favorite subject in school. I was always fascinated with looking at maps (before Google Earth became popular) and saying to myself, I want to go there when I grow up, and I will live here for this period, and then I want to travel to this location. I quickly memorized cities and country locations, while others found geography difficult or unappealing.

However, I wish geography was heavily influenced and taught more in the U.S. school systems. Still, I could be wrong, or we, as Americans, seem to care about something other than geographical locations. Watching videos of Americans being tested on their geography knowledge saddens me, especially when it comes to knowing where all the states, especially the major ones, are located. Some Americans can state the names of celebrities but can't name our country's vice president. How much money would I have made of all the times I heard some Americans not know the actual capital city of the U.S.? Every American should know that and at least know how many stars are on our American flag. It's essential to know the history of the place you live.

It's significantly sad when other nationalities from around the world you've met have more general knowledge of our country than many Americans I've encountered. We were also not taught about the many histories of other countries, except our own countries (but this was based on my school experience alone). I didn't learn much about Canada and the country's evolution in school. Of course, we learned about World War I and II, a little bit of the Cold War, and mostly, about the Revolutionary War and the Civil War. That's it, based on my memories from school, or maybe I wasn't fully attentive and daydreaming of my crush in school instead.

Getting back to my point, we should learn more about geography and know where specific locations and landmarks are in the world, just *in case* we decide to travel. When I first moved to China, a stranger asked me, "Can you see the Great Wall of China from your window?" I was living in Shanghai, and the Great Wall was outside of Beijing. Yes, the Great Wall is long and is visible from space, but the Great Wall didn't extend over to Shanghai. China is a vast country, and the person didn't know and probably was curious, but I may have giggled a bit.

Some people here are less excited about seeing pictures of other places worldwide. I taught a class of third graders, and we played a game to try to guess the continent, country, and place this picture shows. And surprisingly, they were so unenthusiastic. I am still surprised that many students need to learn the names of the continents.

For laughs and entertainment, I love watching YouTube videos of Americans trying to locate specific geographic locations, let alone answering trivia questions about their land. As a kid, schools taught this information; it's general knowledge, but it's only somewhat prevalent now. Fewer Americans could care less about their country's history and knowing where many states are in the U.S.

But I love that navigating the U.S. is so easy because everything is in English. I am not trying to mispronounce street names while navigating in an Uber or taxi. I understand all the street and highway laws and know what to expect here. Even the billboards, signs, and food menus are all in English. I forget the struggle of having my translator app ready to scan the foreign language and translate what it says, especially regarding food. When I visited Japan a couple of years ago, it had the least written English anywhere, but I am unsure if that's the same now. I clearly remember walking in the cities of Japan, trying to understand the Japanese menus because their characters were difficult to read since I couldn't read Japanese. I had to depend on the pictures that matched the characters and hoped for the best. That country was the hardest to navigate, but we made it happen then. Japanese people were so helpful there.

From our experience, when I traveled with some friends, we had the "I don't know where the hell we are going?" look on our faces, and the people living there could sense our lost looks and came up to help us.

As I stated earlier, an adjustment that seemed small but significant was seatbelts. Thank goodness I never got into an accident with the lack of seatbelts overseas or when I was on the back of bikes in Asia. People drive manically through the crowded streets overseas. However, I saw fewer accidents than I did in the United States. I felt that drivers in other countries are so adapted to crazy driving that they're always on high alert and more attentive to decrease their chances of accidents. I'm still trying to figure out how there are more accidents in the States. What do you think?

Since I have not traveled much internationally since moving back home, I'm losing my geographic knowledge! When I lived overseas, I was always looking at maps and planning my next spot to visit. I'm looking at my bank account, praying I can afford another trip outside the States. Many Americans don't fly outside the country because it can be too expensive. The closest places to fly are Mexico, Canada, and Latin America without making a massive dent in their savings. Overseas, it felt so much easier to travel from place to place, and tickets didn't seem unreasonable; plus, you seem to have more comfort in flying with leg space, entertainment, and sometimes the food they provide. In Europe, transportation to travel within the continent is easy and convenient.

Truthfully, it took me a few months to identify and know where Texas's major cities were. Living in Texas can sometimes feel like living in a foreign country. It's massive, too, especially when you decide to drive to another city on the other side of Texas. It can take a whole day to go to one side of Texas! However, Texas is full of neat little towns and views all over the place, and I'm excited to continue to explore this beautiful state! It has so much to offer.

Do you feel the same way? After moving back home, did your traveling days become obsolete?

Chapter 6

Long Time No See!

"Shall I continue my list discussing the difficulty of making friends, confrontations, geography, and so forth? I will spare you my carping. Readjusting to life in the U.S. felt just like when I acclimatized to life in another country. I become hyper-aware of peoples' interactions and differences. I observed the things they said, did, and valued. After my initial weeks and months of reverse culture shock, I learned to take things with a grain of salt and appreciate the "good" in several matters that once frustrated me.

While I clearly took note of all these "unique" characteristics of life on U.S. soil, and they may have a somewhat bitter undertone, there are countless positive reasons why I am pleased with my decision to move back to my home country. I love it, defend it, and wear it proudly despite all this criticism. I have recreated a sense of belonging and know I am in the right place for now."

-Eric, who lived abroad for ten years.

When you visit home after being away for months or even years, you may get the flutter sensation in your stomach and the excitement building up because you're going home to familiar places and faces. There's nothing more invigorating when you have a family member or friend come to meet you at the airport. It's a fantastic feeling to see someone familiar on the other side after a long journey.

After adjusting to being back home for a day or two, you have a long list of things to do and people to see quickly before heading back to your host country. Then catching up with family and friends felt like no time had passed.

Then you have other people who live vicariously through you and your journeys overseas and they usually state how they would love to come to visit you. Nonetheless, that's only sometimes the case. When you come home for a visit, they will tell you they will drive to see you because you're not home often. However, about 95% of the time, people rarely make an effort to drive the distance, a short distance in this matter, to see you. What sucks is when you fly home, and that person who claims they want to catch up with you won't drive even thirty minutes to a few hours to see you, even though you flew halfway across the world. You realize then that you know your true friends, and that they would make the time to see you. After a few trips back home, I realized that no matter the distance you travel, friends will be too busy with their own lives, which is understandable. I just stopped trying to make an effort to reach out to those friends and just focused on spending time with those who genuinely care about me. It's not worth the time and stress.

I'm sure other Americans would fly home to see their loved ones and have had the experience of their friends and family not taking the time to come out and see them while visiting home. Maybe their friends and family will say they will visit wherever they are living, but it's rare when they come to visit them overseas. However, if family and friends come for a visit, it's a fantastic feeling to see someone familiar, and they experience the same thing as their loved one who moved overseas. My family visited me while I lived in China and Egypt, and they thoroughly enjoyed the experiences, especially the food.

Why do many Americans here think living overseas is like living in a warfare zone? It's not. I felt safer over there than I did here. There are many unsafe places to live worldwide, including the United States. I felt less secure here than in major cities in other countries. Yes, theft can happen anywhere and at any time. My house got robbed twice many years ago in the States. Therefore, I was ensured our new security code was always on and everything was constantly locked. I was living in that state of fear. I used to carry pepper spray everywhere, especially walking alone at night. I couldn't even have pepper spray or anything similar in certain countries, but I felt safe most of the time, even at night. I always kept my guard up when I lived abroad because of living in fear back home because of past experiences.

Now that I moved back. I'm still alert to my surroundings and habitually lock my car every time I enter it before leaving the parking lot. It's sad to know that places here can make you feel unsafe.

I still can't believe my chapter overseas went by fast and to this day I reminisce all the great times I had experienced. It's different here. I love my job and being with my husband, but the adventures now differ slightly. Usually, most weekends, I would fly to Singapore or South Korea when living in Asia and Italy when living in Egypt. The cost was the same as flying from Houston to New York City. I don't have the same thrill flying from state-to-state as I did from country-to-country. It's the adventure of exploring a new country, a new language, and trying new foods. Each state is different in the States, but generally, the food is the same, and most people speak English. So, I don't have the same excitement to fly to another state, especially when price tickets are overpriced here, and I refuse to fly a budget airline here. Do you feel the same way?

How would you feel if you were one of the Americans who left everything behind because you had a once-in-a-lifetime experience in another country? I didn't think twice and just took the leap when I received my first international job offer. I was going through life changes and wanted a fresh start, and this opportunity came at the perfect time. Life is too short, and if you said no, who knows what experiences you would have missed out on. I'm sure you had doubters who thought you were crazy and insane to move from a place you knew and how safe it is here than there. It's scary to move your entire life abroad, but the new opportunities you face could be life-changing and for the better.

I was in my late 20s, in a failed marriage, moved back home with my parents, and needed a fresh start. I didn't like my hometown and wouldn't succeed by staying there. I knew I wanted to live in another country; I didn't know how or where to start. A friend introduced me to a platform where you can find international teaching jobs. I had a few interviews, and, boom, got an offer to teach in China. I remember running downstairs and telling my parents I'm moving to China. Both of my parents were ecstatic for me and encouraged me to go. It was now or never. And it was the best decision I ever made.

Over the last decade, I learned lessons, burned a few bridges, and even rekindled friendships. After all this, I found out who my true, lifelong friends were. That's part of living life. You do find out who is by your side and who has their backs turned against yours. If the other party doesn't put in the effort and constantly pinpoints all the issues on you, you need to cut ties with them and move on; it's not worth the stress.

Chapter 7

Tip Tip Hooray!

"I think tipping here is wrong and a pain in the butt. Frankly, servers and wait staff should be paid a living wage. What annoys me more than anything is when I order food from a restaurant, and it asks me if I want to add a tip. Why? I ordered and picked up the food. Other than that, I've gotten used to automatically adding the 20% despite my hatred. People deserve a living, and I'd happily pay more for my food if it meant that they were getting paid a living wage. Reduce my portion size and pay them a larger wage. With that being said, I rarely go out to eat, and when I do, it's mainly takeout."

-Anne, who lived abroad for eleven years.

Here's another sore subject for people— tipping. Tipping is a definite requirement when receiving almost any kind of service nowadays here in the States. I get it; if you have money to go out to eat, you should be able to tip the server.

On the other hand, when you receive a not-so-great service like my husband and I did in New York, we didn't tip the server well because of the person's attitude, and as a result, the server started shouting at us. If the service here is over-the-top, we will tip them well. But, I'm not too fond of the fact that when I order a tea or coffee, and it's time to pay, the barista will show the screen of the tipping options to choose from below, and the 20% is always the first one to display. There was a sporting event I attended and bought water. The server took the bottled water out from the fridge next to the counter and was still expected to tip. You took a water bottle out and placed it on the counter. How does that qualify to need a tip?

When I get my hair done here every six to eight weeks, I always tip my hairdresser because she does an excellent job. If I get my nails done and the service is amazing, I will tip. Going to my massage place for an hour foot massage, I tip too. I'm more than happy to tip for these kinds of services. I have to be careful of going to these places often because I spend more money than I would make. So, I have to budget carefully and go occasionally for a pedicure or a massage.

I went to a place this year where I didn't tip because the service was horrible, and I don't feel any shame because this place was highly recommended, but when I got there, it was so dirty and unsanitary. Even when I scheduled my appointment, I had to wait almost an hour. I felt rushed when it was finally my turn. The experience was painful and my eyes burned the entire time. The first red flag of this place was that they didn't clean my eyes before touching my lashes.

Where was I?

I got eyelash extensions. I used to get them all the time overseas. I had some uncomfortable times when getting new extensions, but usually, I can zone out and relax while they put on my new eyelashes. But this time, it was excruciating. After I got them done, they did look nice on me but the cost for a one-time application was about $100. I would have paid at most $30 overseas. However, this is America, where services and goods are more expensive.

Firstly, I didn't like how dirty this place was, and two, they asked if I wanted to add a tip for the technician. I said, "No." They gave me the dirtiest look, but I told them this service wasn't worth $100, even after they tried to upsell me for a monthly membership so my refills would be cheaper. It was still about $80 monthly and then I would have to get refills every two weeks. I wasn't going through that experience every two weeks of the glue burning my eyes. No, thank you.

Sometimes when you sign up for these places via email, the companies will send you a coupon for your first visit or receive a discount if you spend this much on one service. I had a coupon from this company, which applied to this situation. However, the cashier replied, "I don't know why our company sends these coupons because we don't allow them at our store." Your store is a chain. If your company sends them, they should allow customers to use the coupons. Otherwise, I no longer want to give my business to this company. That was the last time I would be getting my eyelash extensions for a while. I will stick to glue-ons or magnetics in the meantime.

My husband and I had taken the time to find good restaurants while living in Houston. We succeeded by finding a couple of them. At the same time, we found a few that we won't return to again. One experience, in particular, was a breakfast place. Before trying out a place, we do a Google search and read the reviews, especially the most recent ones. This place had a 4.8-star review, so we gave this place a shot. We still yearned to find the ultimate breakfast place because we love breakfast. We tried this place because they offered healthier, gluten-free, vegetarian, and vegan options. Those specific accommodations reeled me in to try it out. Once we arrived, it looked like a craft store with decor everywhere. They were also renovating and expanding then, so unfortunately, there was a bit of construction and noise, but it was still manageable. When the hostess greeted us, she asked us to pick the various menu options we wanted and to choose a seat. Okay, so far so good.

A major plus to going to this restaurant was that it was open when we arrived there around 9 a.m. on a Saturday. When we seated ourselves, the hostess informed us that when we were ready to order, we could go to the cashier to place what we wanted. We also had to get our drinks at the station and handpick our utensils ourselves. Fair enough. Afterward, I went up to the cashier to give her our order; however, a lady was before me, so I waited for my turn. At that moment, the cashier wasn't paying much attention because she thought the lady in front of me was with me and asked for my order. The cashier accidentally added the lady's order to mine, and thankfully, the cashier returned the order to me before I paid. What sucked the most was that this place gave suggestions for tipping. I felt obligated to click on one of the percentages for the tip, but they didn't provide any waitstaff services; it was an almost self-service place. I could have entered the orders myself, and all they did was bring out the food for me. By not being a jerk, I still gave a percentage tip, but I shouldn't feel obligated to provide a tip when there wasn't excellent service. And most of all, the food was bland.

I made an occasional stop at this restaurant that makes these specific sandwiches. I eat there and place my order at the counter when I see the cashier. All they do is bring the sandwich out to me, and they also expect a tip. At this place, I also have to get up and pick out my eating utensils and get my drink and napkins. The cashier can see if I provided a tip, which, to me, is a personal matter. I didn't tip once, and she turned a one-eighty on me and tossed my sandwich to me while I sat at my table. I shouldn't have to tip if you hand me a sandwich a few feet from the kitchen. The next time I visited, I gave a small tip, and suddenly, the lady was pleasant. I would have searched for an alternative place if it wasn't for this specific sandwich and the location.

As mentioned in a previous chapter about food, my husband and I noticed that the restaurant service has declined, as it used to be different. Was it from the pandemic, or did the U.S. lose some of its service standards? I don't know. The standard wage for food service is still meager, and they need to pay their servers and waitstaff a better salary. I don't get the price gouging of food items at a restaurant or even at a small cafe. We went to a cafe in our home city, found some delicious coffee, and got some basic sandwiches; the total cost was $30! The price tags are mind-boggling, and I get it because of inflation but don't keep raising prices of food and services when the general population can't receive raises that cover the inflation percentage. Many people are also starting to cook and eat meals because it costs an arm and a leg to go out. On average, it would cost us at least $50 for two people, including water and the entree. We rarely buy soda or drinks or even dessert. I could barely afford to eat out more than two times a week. I love to have a night out where I get excellent service, a fantastic meal, and not have to do the dishes, but beggars can't be choosers. In the end, I have saved a bit of money from eating out less.

Living back in the U.S., I don't understand why our dollar bills are the same color and why we still use coins, such as pennies. I have randomly collected change over the years, and now I sit with a pile of change that will only be useful to me if I start digging out my wallet like an old lady and counting my change to give to the cashier. Most places are moving to a cashless system, especially after the pandemic, but I still hate carrying any loose change, since it's hard to get rid of. From time to time, I try to give the exact change when purchasing something at the store because change becomes quite heavy.

The countries with the most beautiful currency I've seen so far are the Hong Kong and the Australian Dollar. I love the colors and that they are very distinctive when telling them apart. They and other currencies are similar to theirs. They remind me of Monopoly money, but I love it. At least it's colorful.

After returning to the U.S., saving money here is so hard. You can, in specific ways, by not eating out, purchasing memberships, or not buying cable. It's the cost of living here that makes it hard to save. Our cost of living keeps increasing at an alarming rate.

When the pandemic started, I wasn't in the U.S. yet, but I had a nice chunk of savings racked up due to everywhere being closed. But when stores started opening in mid-June in Egypt, I felt I was shopping impulsively and was saving less money each month. I fell back into the pit of consumerism.

Most of the savings I earned in Egypt were spent on clothes because I felt I was wearing the same thing every day when teaching online. Being stuck indoors for some time, I needed something to make me feel good: buying clothes. There are better solutions. However, if I could go back to that time, I would have used that money I spent on clothes towards my savings, especially I would have needed it when I moved back to the U.S. Unfortunately, I don't have a housing allowance here anymore, so I have to use a chunk of my paycheck towards the rent.

From tipping to living costs, it's nuts where our money goes and what is expected here in the States. Tipping in some countries is considered rude, while in other countries, it's suggested that you tip. Before I plan for a trip, I would search online to see if it's required to tip because if you don't know, you may get unpleasant glances from the service people. What is your opinion about tipping in the U.S. and or your home country?

Chapter 8

Calls, Apps, Commercials, Advertisements, Oh My!

"When I finally came back to the United States to live and work, it was toward the end of the pandemic; I had one friend, no car, and zero clues about where I was geographically. It was my first week in Houston, Texas, and I felt jet-lagged, weepy, and generally annoyed. I decided to Google the nearest coffee shop, take a walk there, and come back. Walking usually helped with those negative feelings, and coffee was always a good choice.

Not surprisingly, the only walkable coffee location was a Starbucks about two miles away. I begrudgingly got dressed, put on my shoes, and set off. The entire walk was along the massive, beige, seven-lane Katy Freeway. The cars were so loud and

SO big! I was feeling slightly overwhelmed but was already half a mile in, so I continued.

I got to the Starbucks with only two cat calls and one close incident with a guy running a red light as I was about to cross the street. This was a success in my book, and I was in better spirits. As I approached the door to the Starbucks, a sign greeted me, saying, 'Due to the pandemic and shortage of staff, the inside of this location is closed. Please place your order on the Starbucks app or use the drive-thru. Thank you for being so understanding.'"

-Katelyn, who lived abroad for ten years.

Never in my life have I received so many unknown spam callers, not just weekly but daily. I have never seen so many red missed calls on my phone. What has changed in the last few years? There was a website where you could register your number, and the spam callers would stop, but that didn't work; it worsened.

It took me ages to check my voicemail since I got a U.S. number, and I feel horrible for not checking in because I am sure I had essential messages that needed to get through.

As a millennial, I don't like talking on the phone and avoid it if I have to. But I accessed my mailbox, and I had a full one. There were forty-five voicemail messages! I usually have to delete all the unknown numbers on my missed call list almost every week because there are so many. I keep getting those automated messages about seeking financial help. No, thank you. I'm alright, and I will block this number along with the other million numbers I have blocked.

However, it's much easier to text. It's just weird to talk on the phone now, especially when you have conversations through text messaging. When placing a food order on the app overseas, the representative would have to call me to tell me something was out, or I needed a choice, and my anxiety would go through the roof. It's rare to talk on the phone overseas, unless it's someone you know. If you needed to contact someone who didn't speak your language, WhatsApp was ideal because you could easily translate what they said via text. Using iMessage overseas was uncommon, so we would use other social apps.

I'm thankful my phone can pick up a spam caller and save me the time to answer the call here. I usually have the "do not disturb" button on my phone, and I would usually miss these spam calls and not be interrupted throughout the day.

My husband and I contemplated what internet/cable package to get when we settled into our home. Before deciding, I clearly remember when we first came to Florida to stay temporarily with my parents, and the continuous play of commercials with cable was overwhelming.

Any time a commercial comes on, it's either an advertisement for fast food or a pharmaceutical drug you may need if you're experiencing a health issue. Once you're glued to these commercials, the idea of wanting fast food, soda, or ice cream starts popping up. Or you start psyching yourself out thinking, do I have this health issue? Next, you begin to overthink and are in that anxiety panic pit. Then, *BOOM!* You're consuming these items based on temptation. I've read recently on the internet that 70%

of the U.S. economy is on consumer spending. It makes perfect sense since many of our ads are visible everywhere on the internet, on TV, or while driving.

So, my husband and I decided to avoid purchasing cable because it's about $70 or more, and most shows consist of commercials. We will gladly pay for the internet and a subscription to see shows and movies when needed, but save money and avoid purchasing cable. I just realized how almost anything and everything is advertised here, urging others to buy now, or you may regret it. When I feel tempted by these advertisements, I try to distract myself from purchasing something or some service I don't need because I will fall into that black hole of useless consumption.

Another thing I've noticed, or in this case, a strategy many businesses use, is upsells! For example, you take your car just to get an oil change. Minutes later, after the mechanics change your car's oil, they bring up all these "suggestions" that your vehicle will need this or that, and somehow they convince you, then you're leaving the service station with new windshield wipers, brake pads, and brand new tires.

However, if you know how businesses operate despite them trying to convince you that you *need* certain items right away, even if it's hard to say no, don't be afraid to say no.

After living overseas, I've learned to stop buying materialistic items (well, trying to) because we will either, one, try to pack them into our suitcases when moving; two, sell the items because there's no room; or three, end up donating them to someone because we ran out of time. Overall, materialistic things consume too much space and can waste money. I can't tell you how many clothes, souvenirs, bags, and accessories I had to purge, sell, or even donate the time I spent overseas. I regret getting rid of sentimental items or items necessary because I would have to repurchase them in the next country.

Once we started learning these lessons of buying new items, we had to sit and think about whether we truly needed them or not. Will we get our money's worth, or will it be tossed out? It's still been a struggle, but I have held back the temptation mostly because it's undoubtedly not easy when you can access everything in this country.

Chapter 9

The New Me

"Today, I saw another friend post on Facebook that their summer holiday in the USA was over, and they were returning to their host country. This used to be me. The person who stocked up on memories with friends and family and, just as important, all the American goods I could fit in my bags before leaving for a home on another continent. For over a decade, I was this person. Now, here I am, sitting on my new couch, inside my new apartment, in a new city in the States, feeling inundated by waves of sadness and envy. I've relocated to three countries in twelve years, and this is the first time I've doubted a decision to move. I guess it's time to buckle in because I am officially on track to repatriate, so the real adventure is about to begin."

-Diana, who lived abroad for twelve years.

Moving back permanently and knowing you're not on vacation anymore can feel surreal. Deep down, you may think you wish you were returning to your host country with your entire stock of items you need until your next trip back home. The summer I moved back, my friends were visiting home for a few weeks, and then I saw on social media that they were excited for their next chapter, new country, and new position overseas. It stung a bit because I was that person. I stayed behind and they were heading off to their new adventure. You feel jealousy starting to creep in, but you're back in your home country, a place where you don't have to stress whether you can speak the language or have to learn a new culture all over again.

Once I settled into my new home and city, I realized most conversations are surface-level and usually circle around houses, babies, new cars, and which sports team won last night. It sometimes feels very cookie-cutter, but it doesn't mean it's terrible. But sometimes, it can feel like Groundhog Day, where the cycle never ends.

But you can't get mad if you and specific people don't see eye-to-eye. It is frustrating when you are talking about travels, trying new cuisines, or having a unique experience; some seem to care initially but then lose interest and return to mundane conversations. However, I will give people here this: they try to understand and ask questions about overseas travel, but it's not their fault that they don't understand those who have lived abroad. That was something I had to accept and live with it.

We are becoming less social due to the pandemic, or maybe it's because we have a phone attached to our hands and rather text instead of talking or calling people. Even now, I prefer texting and feel awkward talking on the phone with someone. I feel like a robot when answering customer service, and they probably think I don't know how to put sensible words in a sentence. Honestly, I don't like it because I talk to people, even strangers, but it feels weird, and instead of saying, here's a text, I think it's easier. Is this the road we are going down as humans?

Then, I feel like an alien when conversations start popping up around other people. If the other party is interested in any topic I bring up, I second-guess myself that isn't the American norm. I have caught myself judging myself when the other person is not interested in anything I bring up, and I end up making the conversation awkward. The truth is making small talk is easy but it can take a lot of energy since I'm an introvert.

I had a daily conversation about mediocre food, and I was to the point: is this the norm? How is this topic benefiting me in some way? Sitting there with the other party, thinking, do we have anything else to discuss? Is this the norm in the U.S.? I love talking about what's happening outside of our work lives, especially when I consider my weekends and evenings golden times and choose not to do school work during those times. I take my breaks very seriously and work my tail off during work hours to get everything checked off my to-do list.

It's difficult not to eavesdrop on other people's conversations, especially when they are loud and maybe want others to hear, but you can't help but chuckle at some of the conversations that come from people. It's unbelievable to think you can understand many people in this country and can feel overwhelmed.

I encountered a lady who lives here who told her daughter, who was visiting from another state, bluntly stating, "She needs some sun because she looks pale from living in Colorado." She judged her daughter because she wasn't tan and the lady looked like an old leather handbag. I forgot how much getting tanned is a priority in the U.S. If you don't have a tan, you look sickly. I even succumbed to using a tanning bed to get my base color so I wouldn't burn as much in the natural sun. That was another dumb decision I've ever made. I stopped using tanning beds and baking in the sun after I worked in the dermatology field and didn't care if I got the perfect tan each summer. I've seen so much skin cancer, which made me rethink getting out in the sun for a nice tan. Plus, I aged much faster because of the sun damage. When I moved to Asia, I noticed that it was okay to look pale, and many followed those tracks. Whereas, in the States, pale is not the norm. Since I moved here, people have commented on my skin's fairness; it's pretty annoying.

I have been in social situations where if people I don't know won't greet me at all, well, I must be the one to initiate, which is okay because people can be shy and not extroverted. And I'm the farthest from being an extrovert. However, I display kindness by asking the person's name and getting to know them a bit. Many keep their guard up, which makes it challenging to get to know them. As time passes, such as at birthday parties, where you just met these strangers, you want to get to know them because it would be awkward the whole time. You also want to avoid spoiling a friend's birthday party by not being the jerk who doesn't want to socialize with the friend's party guests. It's sad to see the other party not reciprocating the "getting to know you" questions and just finding ways to veer away from you, leaving you standing by yourself, looking foolish. I feel it's pretty rude that everyone should buck up, be adults, and try to be pleasant to others at any social event. You can tell the tenseness or the awkwardness when others don't want to engage with you in conversation. It's like a label slapped across our foreheads that says, "Hello I'm a repatriate and I don't fit in here anymore."

It's hard to fit back into your home country, catch up on events you've missed, mend bridges that were once collapsing, and make up for lost time, but sometimes the effort isn't enough. We may not be the same as we first left our home, but we still want to feel included and heard.

Also, making new friends is a hundred times harder as you get older, and trying to blend in as a chameleon isn't as easy as one would think. But you can sense when those other people who have been in the same city for years don't take newcomers, even if you have the same nationality.

I often follow a specific podcast, and this host said something that resonated with me. He said some people are batteries, while others are vacuums. When you hang around people who are batteries, they give you energy after hanging out with or talking to them. You feel energized and positive. Then you have the vacuums—those who suck the energy out of you. When hearing this, I reflected on myself by questioning whether I was a battery or a vacuum. It depends on the day and who I'm around. Nobody wants to be a vacuum, but sometimes we become this way without realizing it. I learned that I want friends who want to help and support me. So, as an adult, I'm becoming more aware of who I surround myself with so I don't become a vacuum myself. I am a vacuum sometimes; however, a swift kick in my butt helped me realize there is so much to be grateful for, and I need to be a battery for others.

Overall, I have accepted this new chapter in my life, continuing to adjust to my home country despite its obstacles, the awkwardness of meeting new people, and how days can feel like Groundhog Day. It's becoming the new norm, the new me.

Chapter 10

Doctor, Doctor, Where Are You?

"Finding doctors through different portals here and there stressed me out. Why can't I go to one place, book an appointment without going through the entire consultation process, and see another doctor after the green light? Insurance here is just expensive, and you are lucky if you can get an appointment as soon as you can. Sometimes, I had to wait a month because of no availability."

-Ana, who lived abroad for seven years.

Panic started rising because I was nervous that my overseas health insurance was expiring on July 31st. We were moving to the States in mid-July, and I wasn't going to start my new job until the end of July and my new insurance wouldn't kick in until mid-August. So, I was praying hard for no health issues or accidents.

I was overwhelmed when I had to select my vision, dental, and healthcare insurance plans and whether to choose the PPO (Preferred Provider Organization) route or the HSA (Health Savings Account) route. I didn't know the difference between a PPO plan and a HSA plan until I had to research it. I remember I had to choose about eleven plans, and the total cost for my husband and myself to be on my insurance was ridiculously expensive! I never had to calculate the amount taken out of my paycheck from my health insurance, compared to what I experienced overseas. I wasn't sure if I could even see the total amount of health insurance deducted from my overseas salary.

Ultimately, I was spending an arm and leg for health insurance here and wanted to faint. And the health insurance's copay and deductible still didn't make sense to me, especially after how much we spend on monthly health insurance. My husband had to be on my health insurance because he couldn't work because he didn't have a work visa since he's not American. We decided to apply for a green card in late October 2021 so he could eventually work.

When it was time for the routine check-ups, I forgot the endless wait to see the doctors here, even with an appointment. I don't understand why they tend to book patients and eventually you're waiting around for at least an hour or more. Then when you think the wait is over, no, you have to wait even more in the doctor's room, sitting in a paper drape where your arse and body are freezing to death while awkwardly waiting around for someone to enter the room. I loathe going to my yearly check-ups with the gynecologist and the dentist. Those two make my blood pressure spike up.

After the initial shock of having to pay for health insurance, especially when dental and vision aren't included with the general healthcare, I still wasn't a fan of why we still pay copays and get slapped with a bill a few months later. I realized it depends on the amount on your deductible. While growing up in the States, I was never taught or explained why this system works this way. Why wasn't I taught the difference between PPO and the

HSA, and which plan would benefit me more? Don't even get me started about the health insurance cost here. This and learning how to do your taxes, make investments, and many more would be beneficial to know before becoming an adult.

We also decided to get pet insurance because vet visits here are expensive. It's been challenging to find a suitable vet for our cats because each one we've tried didn't seem to love their jobs as vets and always gave us attitudes and restated that my cat wasn't a good patient and always needed a relaxer before any appointment. Then we get charged for vet assistance because my cat was being too "difficult," I'm assuming. We miss our amazing vet in Egypt, who was a rare gem, and he truly loved his job. He helped our cats for three years and never had an issue with my cat being too aggressive. Just like dental insurance for humans, it's not much better for pets. Teeth cleaning is more expensive for pets than it is for humans. The vet clinic in Texas quoted me for one of my cats for a dental cleaning, tooth extraction, blood tests, etc., roughly $1000!

I went to a dentist for a check-up since my last cleaning was in Egypt. I have had dental issues ever since I was a kid, which were out of my control, but now I have to face the reality that I need to maintain my dental health. In this dentist's office, while you're sitting on the infamous torture chair waiting for the dental hygienist and dentist to evaluate your mouth, I overhear other clients receiving their estimated amount of what they would have to pay out of pocket for their dental procedures. Even with dental insurance, many procedures aren't covered. Over the last year, I had to set extra money aside to pay for an upcoming dental procedure that dental insurance would not cover. I have also talked to others asking how their dental insurances work in other countries, and I have concluded that dental insurance is not a priority for humans.

Overseas has flaws too, especially with doctor visits. We either had to pay an amount up front, instead of getting billed. If you didn't have the chunk of money for a procedure or surgery, you would have to borrow or use your credit card. Getting X-rays, scans, and other tests was cheaper than in the States.

A friend of mine had to get surgery done, and the upfront cost where she lived was at least $12,000 and no one usually had that much money to pay upfront at that time. So, there can be a downfall with having health insurance overseas.

Luckily, in my overseas experiences, I was fortunate to have health insurance, which I paid upfront. Then, a few weeks later, I got reimbursed with the exact amount from the insurance company. I do miss that aspect of living abroad.

I moved abroad for two reasons: to travel the world and to save more money. I have always persuaded teachers and other professionals to move overseas because the money is good in most places, and you can save. I can make more in the U.S., but the taxes and living costs affect my salary tremendously. Teaching overseas, you would get housing pay (depending on the package and the country) that would match what you pay for rent, a ticket to fly home each year, and even a signing-on bonus if you extend your contract (in most international schools). Many places in Europe are where teachers would love to go; I mean, who can blame them? The international packages aren't the best for teachers in Europe, and saving money is much more challenging. The Middle East and Asia are the top two places to save if you need to rack up a good chunk of savings in a short amount of time. However, I'm sure the international packages have changed since COVID-19, so this was based on my pre-COVID experiences.

Chapter 11

Where Did That Price Come From?

"We were immediately overwhelmed by the prices of everything. When it was time to look for our first American apartment together, we budgeted $700. We thought that would be a fair price considering we had zero furniture and wanted nothing more than a small, happy apartment in the middle of town. We didn't even want a dining room! The day we started looking, reality set in. If we wanted to pay that little for an apartment, not only would we still get a dining room we didn't want, but we would also be sacrificing our safety. The crime rates across the U.S. are not pleasant, but we noticed any apartment we viewed in the $700 range also included a higher-than-usual crime rate. It's disappointing and sad, for sure. So, ultimately, we ended up upping our budget to $1000,

which afforded us a 650-square-foot apartment with NO dining room (yay!) In the center of town. Even more importantly, it was part of a gated apartment community which we began to realize was very important to us."

-Emily, who lived abroad for six and a half years.

Oh! How do I remember the cost of items, plus tax, here?

Look at that sale!

That is a reasonable price; there's a sales tax. What's the sales tax?

I have to remember which state I am in.

Let me Google it. Thank goodness for quick searches on Google.

The downfall of our price tags is that there is no included tax. Then, we have to do the mental calculation or wait for the swift punch in the stomach of the final total on the cash register. And the sales tax isn't the same across the United States; it's all different. Then I hear there is no sales tax in Alaska. Move there, maybe not? Scratch that; too cold for me!

Anyway, I like it when the price is upfront, in black and white, so I can calculate how much I will be spending, especially at a store in the mall. The shopping in Egypt was terrific, with malls galore, and they had almost everything you needed except the occasional quality makeup products.

When you come back for visits, it's different because you buy necessary items (or stock up on items) because countries may not have those specific things you're looking for. For example, a good face wash that doesn't bleach your skin, or delicious home snacks you crave, such as Butterfingers, chocolate-covered raisins, and even alcohol! Each time I came home, I brought two suitcases, one always empty, so I could fill up my supplies while visiting home. I swear, shoes would take up the most room in bags, and shampoo and conditioner because I need a color-safe shampoo that works specifically on my hair. I wasn't successful with hair products overseas. I spent at least a grand on shoes, clothes, makeup, skincare, spices, and food when I came back home for my yearly visit. It was hard to find shoes in my size. Shoes in Asia were much smaller and the quality I would find wasn't always the best. I did buy these gorgeous sequin flats in Asia and unbelievably, they were my size and lasted a year or so. Currently, I can search in my closet and find one pair of shoes I have bought while living overseas, whereas the others were purchased in one of the States. Not to mention, buying shoes online here was too easy and dangerous at times, especially when there were sales. I was converting my U.S. shoe size to U.K. size because everyone was using the U.K. sizing.

Before heading back to my host country, I would stop at a specific cosmetics store and come out with new makeup and accessories, spending at least $200-$300 on average each time. It seemed like a lot of money but the makeup would last for almost a year. I still love the store, but all I see now are dollar signs everywhere. There are so many face creams, makeup items, and hair accessories, and they all do the same thing. So many competitive cosmetic products, and sadly, I have tried the hype items and ended up with disappointment. One doesn't work better than the other, especially the face creams. It's unimaginable that these items are too overpriced, and we will gladly spend several dollars to purchase what we see that makes us feel beautiful. I still need to understand why foundations and concealers are expensive. I bought them before, and I don't wear them daily because I feel heavy with foundation or contour cream, and I tend to look like a clown. I am sure those who use it do it well, but people are beautiful with natural beauty. I also become overwhelmed with the vast amount of beauty products they have there, and I can spend hours and still be indecisive about which lipstick looks better on my skin tone. Now, when I buy a refill on makeup, I'm more cautious of not overspending and reminding myself that I can visit this store any time than the once-a-year visit.

Additionally, all the mascaras work the same for me. I have spent too much money on "luscious" and "lengthy" eyelash mascaras that did nothing but create more clumps on the lashes. Go for the slightly cheaper, vegan-friendly options; you will save your pocket of spending and help the environment and animals.

Also, know your skin type. Your skin may react differently if you live in different climate regions. For example, I lived in a highly humid climate, and my skin was already dry. So, my skin would react differently to the creams I used, versus when I lived in the extremely dry, with no humidity, I would have to use an alternative face cream to maintain the moisture barrier on my face.

Whenever I go to a retail store here, I get the constant automatic response of the cashier asking, "Would you want to save an additional 20% off on today's purchases if you sign up for our rewards credit card?"

"No, thank you," is my immediate response.

But that's how consumerism gets you. You feel that you got these fantastic deals, and then at the end, they throw you an additional discount to save even more if you sign up for their store credit card. It's tempting, but I'm not here to spend more money on another credit card. Let me pay for the items I want, and I'm okay not saving an additional 20% today.

Another cost that shocked me was the amount of tax added to the final cost of either your hotel stay or an Airbnb. I would find this fantastic deal and think that's the final total. Nope, it's not the final price because there is an included tax, cleaning services, and other fees tacked onto the cost of the nightly stay. Both hotels and Airbnbs are over-the-top expensive here! We paid over $400 for one night in a New Orleans Airbnb, and it wasn't worth the nightly price. We paid the included cleaning fee and still felt that the place was quite dirty. We haven't used Airbnbs since that experience.

Overseas, I didn't have the crazy added tax. Most of the time, the total cost was transparent when selecting how many nights you stayed at this resort, which helped me plan and budget accordingly.

The prices of Uber and Lyft are also high here, especially when the prices surge at different times of the day. It happened overseas, too, but I could get an Uber ride from my neighborhood, which was on the right side of the Cairo area, and go to Giza, which was about 44 km (27 miles), and it cost no more than 150 EGP (around $8)! It would cost at least $45 if I took the same distance trip to somewhere in Houston. However, I have dealt with horrible drivers overseas who would cancel me at the last minute or need help to "find" my current pick-up location, and it was frustrating at times.

We only took a few Ubers or Lyfts while living in Houston until we could get a car. The amount we would spend on rides, especially in the area where I lived, the cost of rides would equal up to about my monthly car payment. It was best to get a car when we settled in Houston as soon as possible. Thankfully, a friend lent us a car because I had to commute to work and Ubers would have been an exorbitant amount of money.

Prices have changed a lot since I left the States years back, and now things have become too expensive, and you can spend too much money if you're not careful. Buying clothes at the malls overseas was easy. It's much easier here, and I can spend hundreds of dollars in a few minutes, whether online or in stores. I am also cautious of spending money on things I don't always need now, but I am trying to think more long-term than short-term because I want to save my money as much as I can for future trips, a possible move, and retirement.

Chapter 12

You Can't Sit with Us!

"A huge area of reverse culture shock my husband, and I experienced was the lack of open social community here in the U.S., or at least where we moved. But I remember this when I lived in Raleigh, too; it was part of why I was ready to move to China. When we moved here, we were eager to make friends and start the robust social life we were used to in Asia. We were used to moving to a new city, meeting friends from work and the community immediately, and making best friends for life straight away. Everyone in the international community was so welcoming and excited to have new friendships. Because if you are a Westerner moving to Asia, you might also be a Type 7 Enneagram like my husband and I, eager to meet people and have new experiences. Maybe we were all the same over there.

Whatever the case, it was the opposite experience in Charlotte. We are happy now, 4 1/2 years in, but it took us over a year to feel like we finally had some real friends in Charlotte. It was extremely difficult to make our way into any friendship circle. It just didn't feel like anyone here wanted to meet someone new. It felt like they were content with the same people they had known for 15 years and had no use for us. We finally connected with more of the transplants to Charlotte, who also didn't have pre-existing friendships to rely on, and we got closer to people at work. It was hard, though. So it is much harder than making friends overseas!"

-Emily, who lived abroad for six and a half years.

As I stated before, finding and making new friends is even harder when you're an adult. If you grew up in the same town or lived in a specific place for an extended period, you have more of a chance to have long-lasting friendships since everyone knows you. If you have moved around like I did, creating, building, and maintaining relationships are more difficult for me. I'm sure others who read this feel the same way, especially if you have moved around a lot.

My family and I had to move right at the end of my junior year in high school, and let me tell you, at that time, it was such a terrible time for me. I lived in this previous town since I started preschool and stayed there until we moved down south. Moving right before your senior year was hard as hell. I had to make the best of what I could for the last academic school year, trying to make friends during my senior year, which was nearly impossible because I was off to college the following year. Trying to fit in and make friends in the South differed from living in the North. After many years living in this state, I still felt misplaced and that since I was a northerner, I would never fit into the southern lifestyle and would never have that southern "look." Why I say this is because someone I knew told me this. I should have taken this person's comment with a grain of salt, but maybe it had some hidden truth.

On the other hand, one of the best parts of moving overseas is the close-tight communities. No matter where you are from, when you move to a new place or country, many community members, especially the locals, are so inviting. You feel a part of a community, and friendships are easier to make. When you move, you have no pre-judgment on anyone by giving everyone a fresh, clean start. Over time, you make new friendships and build trustworthiness again. The downfall of making new friends overseas is that you or your friends will likely move. But the upside to this situation is you can always visit them in their hometown or wherever they move.

I love the expat communities because everyone is like family. The possibility of hosting events and activities or being invited to them is high in the expat communities. Everyone wants to do something together and it's a great way to bond. Sometimes, during the beginning of the second or third years in the same country as a teacher, cliques officially start to form, and it can be hard to make new friends, or you may not mesh with the new incomers. You're golden as long as you have a friend or two at your beck and call, especially when situations you face overseas can be stressful. Also, it's wise to build friendships with the locals too. They also long to make friends, and guess what? They are the experts in their country, and if you need help, they most likely will give their shirt off their back (not literally) and be there when you need their help. Plus, having a translator always helps. I do miss my overseas friends.

I met my two best friends when I first moved abroad, and I met one of them during the first week of the new teacher orientation. She lived in China a year and a half before I arrived. We clicked automatically; we were single, young, and wanted to travel. We got to know each other and our ways of traveling. We are planners, so she is the perfect traveling buddy. If you're a traveler and you find a buddy to travel with, keep traveling with them. If they know you and you understand how they travel, then it's a perfect match! My best friend is still my traveling buddy to this day.

My other best friend, I keep in touch often even though we are in different parts of the world. We met in China, where she was on my team in the elementary department, and I was very jealous of her when she came because of all the cool ideas she brought to the table and knew how to engage her students. Long story short, my jealousy turned into amazement at how much of an excellent teacher she was, and I was very insecure. We became friends, but it was when we both lived in Egypt (it wasn't planned) that we became best friends. It's unbelievable where life brings us and whose paths you cross wherever you are. As I mentioned before, the international teaching community is a small one. When you and your best friend were in different countries after China and found out you both will move to Cairo, teaching at the same company, which were sister schools, it's wild to think that you believe this person is supposed to stay in your life. When life gives you special people, please keep them in your life. Nourish those friendships and relationships.

Some friends you make along your traveling or moving journey come and go, while others stay put. You also learn valuable lessons about yourself and what your boundaries are as a person. Also, you know how much time you want to invest in other people.

I realized I was more of an introvert than an extrovert. For a long time I thought I was an extrovert. However, I became mentally drained when I spent time with people at events. I loved it, but afterward, I just wanted to crawl into my hermit shell, watch movies, and recharge my battery. But when the pandemic hit, being an introvert wasn't an issue since being by yourself most of the time or with your husband; in this matter, it didn't affect me until being stuck together 24/7 at home. I am still an introvert, but I longed to go outside, see others, and spend time with friends. I go out and see others and then return home to my cocoon to recharge.

More and more people seem to distance themselves and prefer to stay within their comfort zone or are just too tired or too busy to hang out with others here in America. Most weekends, people do their things or don't want to leave their homes. I find it difficult always to contact colleagues or friends to arrange dates with them. It's more often that I reach out to them first than they reach out to me. Overseas, I would always go out with friends and colleagues, from movies to weekend trips.

I learned to be okay with initiating meetups and video calls with friends now. I get that everyone is busy, and they would spare time to catch up with me when we discuss dates to hang out or talk.

I also wonder how couples who meet other couples try to bond new friendships with them, especially if they are on different wavelengths or chapters—hearing that people can use dating apps such as Bumble, Tinder, etc., to meet friends and not for dating. It's hard to meet people nowadays, especially after the pandemic and moving back to a country where many have formed friendships and prefer to keep their circles tight and small. Trying to break that small circle is nearly impossible.

After living in Houston for two years, my husband and I found a group of fantastic people and clicked. Our small circle of friends is sufficient, and I am okay with this for the remainder of our stay in Houston, for however long it might be.

I have learned to cherish my friendships with people worldwide and stay in touch with them as much as possible. They are like my new family, who aren't related by blood. You have pieces of your heart worldwide; there is no better feeling.

Chapter 13

Did That Just Happen?

"As I patiently waited for the cars to move up, a couple of older men walked out of the shop next to Starbucks and saw me standing in the drive-thru. I felt their eyes on me and hoped they would continue walking and mind their business. Instead, true to the fashion of most older white American men, they chose to interact with me.

"Well, hey there!" I heard in a deep southern twang. "You're just standing in the drive-thru?!" the man exclaimed at me. I looked over, smiled, and returned to the car before me.

"I bet your husband would think this is the most in line you've ever been!" he shouted at me with a laugh. The cowboy-esq-looking man next to him laughed joyfully at this clever little joke.

I was driving to a store one day to do some administrative work. Walking in and minding my business, I paid for the documents I had to send when it was my turn at the counter. Two men, one older and one younger, came in that exact order. The younger man flips his lid because the older man cut him off and took his parking spot right out front of the store. There were a few parking spots right in front of the store, but I parked further away to avoid crazy nuts speeding through the parking lot.

The young man caused a commotion in the store for all of us to hear. He told the older man, "Hey man, you didn't have to steal the parking spot I would use. Didn't you see my turn signal? That's why I had a turn signal!"

The older man replied, "Oh, I didn't see you there." He spoke calmly, versus the other man.

"Yes, you did! I can't believe you are that selfish to take a parking spot. You zipped right in there even though I had a turn signal on!"

"I am sorry, sir, but I don't remember seeing you."

In the end, the younger man wouldn't let it go while the other man grumbled. I just shook my head discreetly, and the cashier could read my face of disbelief at what was happening from two kids arguing over a silly parking spot. If this is what a first-world problem is, then this is the perfect example. Many people seem to rush or be in a hurry all the time. I don't get it. There's more to life than arguing who was there first.

We lived in Egypt for three years. I had such a wonderful time during my first year. Moving to a new country gives you that fresh start, full of countless opportunities. I had a great year as a teacher at my new school; I loved the team I worked with and got to explore many places within Egypt. If you have yet to go to the Red Sea, you must. The only time I would return is to see the Red Sea again. It's gorgeous, and to have the opportunity to snorkel or dive there, you would be blown away by what sea life you would see. My most memorable times swimming at the Red Sea were seeing sea turtles and swimming with the dolphins. Of all the seas and oceans I got to swim in, the Red Sea is, by far, the most transparent waters I have seen.

As you know, when you start adjusting to a new country, you begin to find things that annoy you, and everything you see around you gets under your skin, and then you may start to dislike or hate certain aspects of it. It happened to me in all the countries I lived in. There were days I was annoyed with how things operated and other days I loved living there. Eventually, you become numb at the situations that annoy you and have to power through and remind yourself that no place is perfect. I wish I had that mindset more often when I lived overseas. Most of the time, I took many moments for granted and looked at the glass half empty.

One thing that got under my skin while overseas was the waiting game to obtain my resident permit. My school handled our visa paperwork, and I was told I would get a work visa or a resident permit once I arrived in Egypt. When arriving in Cairo, you can quickly enter Egypt with a tourist visa by purchasing it at the counter. It was $25 for a single entry, valid for only 30 days. However, I learned later that you could pay them in EGP (Egyptian Pounds) instead of USD, but they preferred the dollar, but you would have to do a bit of slick arguing. The good thing about my school was that you pay the visa fee and get reimbursed the same amount in USD, not EGP. During my holiday breaks, I left the country to visit nearby places, and each time I returned to Egypt, I had to buy a brand new tourist visa. Each visa would take up half a page, but since Egypt is peculiar about how you put your visas in your passport, you can only put one tourist per page, not two. So, that's a waste of a page in your passport. They needed the other half of the page to stamp the arrival date when you arrived in the country. So, after two years of traveling around, my passport was overloaded with Egyptian tourist visas.

After my second year in Egypt, I still needed to get my resident permit and continued to purchase a tourist visa each time I reentered. The reason I couldn't obtain a resident permit is that the Human Resources in my school kept claiming that my degree didn't state "English" on it, which I knew wasn't true because my degree is a Master's in Elementary Education, like most of the teacher population at my school. I stirred some water with the HR every few weeks. I bugged them continuously until they took action steps to acquire my resident permit. Otherwise, I would still have been entering the country with numerous tourist visas if it wasn't for me pressing down hard on them to get my resident permit. They would only do something once you forcefully told them this is a considerable problem treating your staff.

Right at the start of my second year, we had the new incoming staff, and they received their resident cards within a month of arriving in Egypt, and I was still stuck with nothing. At this point, it was my breaking point of whether I would stay for a third year. I wanted to avoid the hassle of paying for a tourist visa each time, and also, you pay a fine for overstaying the visa, which is forty-five days, not thirty days. The overstaying of your tourist visa's cost was 1500 EGP, about $82. Even though the school reimbursed me for this, I still shouldn't have had to wait two years to get a work visa or a resident permit, which would have saved headaches because they had to keep completing the paperwork to reimburse me for the visas and the overstay fines. If I had not pushed HR to get my residence card, I would still use many more passport pages with 30-day tourist visas. After a long and trying haul of two and a half years, I finally got my residence card.

When I got my residence card, it wasn't an easy process, but a complex one. So, the HR staff at this job couldn't get the residence card without your presence at the government office. Therefore, I had to take a few hours off of work to go with them to this crowded, sweaty government office where I couldn't tell you which floor we had to go on because this place was confusing to go around, especially if you have to go from one floor to another. Before entering the building, there were separate metal detectors for men and women.

After following our HR representative through this building entrance, we would sit in this tiny waiting area with hundreds of people swarming around, many from different countries. It wasn't fun when COVID happened because many didn't wear masks, and you hoped to avoid catching it there. When it was our turn to go up to the window counter, we had to do fingerprints. Surprisingly, we had to get our fingerprints submitted electronically rather than doing it the old route. However, this electronic system took forever to scan your fingerprints. If you scanned your hand across too fast or too slow, it wouldn't capture your prints. Also, you had to press down all your might with your four fingers to finish the fingerprint system. The person behind the counter is yelling at you in Arabic, and you have no idea what they're saying. After doing this process a million times, the scan picked up my fingerprints.

Once you have your fingerprints, you must wait another hour or two in this other sardine location to take your photo. That part was simple, but if no one was working at this station, you had to wait until someone showed up, and there, no one was in a hurry. Finally, you achieved the final step but must wait a few days to receive the residence card. We had to go to these locations on different floors, and if I had to retrace my steps, I would be lost.

It felt like Wonka's golden ticket when I finally had the card. After fighting for over two years, I got my residence card. Sadly, I had to repeat this process not long after because the residence card is only valid for six months.

Having the residence card made a difference because now I had one less thing to worry about when reentering Egypt: not getting charged with a fine or adding another tourist visa to my passport. It made traveling fun again.

So, I've learned in the last country that if you want to get something done, you have to be stern but friendly at the same time. Otherwise, being unassertive doesn't get you anywhere or what you need.

I wanted to tell you a funny story when I first arrived in Egypt. I have many "Did that just happen?"

stories that I'd experienced here, but then you would never finish this book. Before I tell you this embarrassing story, I would love to hear more about these stories from you, and I'll share my email in the last chapter.

If you're preparing for your next move or travel, check if tap water is drinkable. I learned this the hard way. Before drinking any tap water, always boil the water before drinking, or when in doubt, drink filtered water.

Right off the bat, I knew not to brush my teeth with the tap water until my stomach adjusted. Others have used bottled water each time they had to brush their teeth. In the countries before Egypt, I always used tap water but never swallowed any of it while brushing my teeth.

Occasionally, maybe after a good day, you shower and enjoy the water pressure. Before you know it, you're Charlotte in *Sex and the City*, who opens her mouth and the water accidentally pours into her mouth. I had a Charlotte moment. It didn't hit me until I was done showering and I never thought twice about it because it was just a little water, no biggie.

Big mistake. It wasn't long after I realized I should have been more careful. As someone would say, in Egypt, you had the mummy tummy. My first initial thought would mean that someone was pregnant. No, it meant diarrhea for days. It was horrible and it took over a week for my stomach to return to normal. With the triple-digit heat and trying to find a new apartment, it wasn't the best start to our Egypt chapter.

I know many people don't drink from the tap in Houston, but I've done it for the last few years and never had the mummy tummy. The water tastes different, and people say it's not good drinking water in Houston, but I use the tap if I need to drink. Don't worry; we bought a water filter for drinking.

I've learned my lesson on this, and no matter where I travel, I will use bottled water at first when brushing my teeth or thoroughly spit out the water. As for showering, I know if I have thoughts of opening my mouth, I have to take a second to think where I'm at.

Chapter 14

Tips to Moving Back Home

"I was lucky to have my mom here and friends willing to support me. My mom helped me get a car, which was huge. I never expected her to do that, but she did. People don't account for the sheer expense of things when coming home. Unless you're coming home to a storage unit of everything you need for a house or shipping everything from overseas, I was shocked by how much I needed to buy. Three years later, I still feel like I'm catching up; purchasing a house put a kink in that. If I were to recommend anything to expats returning to the U.S., start thinking about returning home. It would be a good start to purchase and send personal items to your parents' house or somewhere else for storage as soon as you decide to move back home. The costs pile up. Another great suggestion would be to have your relatives or friends

-Anne, who lived abroad for eleven years.

I am saving the last chapter for tips and recommendations that may help prepare you if you're moving back to America in the next few weeks, months, or even a year from now. I asked my acquaintances and friends for their tips, not only from my perspective. I hope you'll find these tips beneficial. On the other hand, you can take these tips with a grain of salt.

Tip #1: Save up your earnings as much as you can! You will need a chunk of savings to pay rent or buy a house or car. I had easily spent $6000 on necessities, a month's deposit for our apartment, a down payment on our car, and furniture since places are not all furnished! Be prepared to go into debt due to the upfront costs of necessary items. If you make it without obligation, you're terrific at handling finances. The book *The Total Money Makeover* by Dave Ramsey was a gold mine for rethinking my money, and he advises on having emergency funds, as well as saving three to six months in case of accidents, job losses, death, etc. A vast safety net put me at peace, especially since I had a good chunk of savings. But be prepared to budget, I mean budget, especially since the cost of living is higher and having no housing allowance (if you're a teacher moving from overseas and you received a housing package) in the U.S. affects your monthly salary. I would have saved so much money if my school had provided a housing allowance, but now I have to be extra careful with my budget. If you rent an apartment, expect a percentage to jump (small or large) by the time you decide to renew your lease. After our first year, our monthly apartment cost went up 9%! We didn't expect to see it skyrocket that much. The first year, our rent went up $200 (monthly), based on the "market value."

Tip #2: I recommend looking into a fairly used car if you're returning home temporarily or for a few years. You want to avoid getting stuck with a ridiculous car payment. I recommend purchasing a used vehicle using CarMax, Vroom, or Carvana. We were searching forever for the best-used car with low mileage and within our budget. Then we found our car on Vroom! Vroom was a good place because they did everything for us and delivered the vehicle to our home!

Tip #3: Take some time to shop for car insurance. Look at insurance companies that will also give you cheaper rates if you purchase renter's insurance. Contemplating renter's insurance companies was something new to me when moving to Texas. Some car insurance companies offer discounts if you use them for your renter's insurance (only if you rent a home or an apartment). Unfortunately, I bought my renter's insurance and car insurance from two separate companies. If I had known sooner, I would have gotten a discount when combining the two insurances to get a better deal.

Tip #4: Another related tip to cars. Don't buy an extended warranty when purchasing a used car. Just don't. You might as well throw your money out the window. The extended warranties for a used car are entirely worthless. Take your time finding a car. Many people suggested buying a brand new car because of the "added" warranty, which makes sense, but then you will have a higher car payment. Technically, it's your choice and what fits best for your budget. If you have a good chunk of money, put that down towards your down payment, decreasing your monthly payments. Remember that most car loans stretch out over 72 months or six years.

Tip #5: If you have the funds, hire movers! If you are moving apartments or moving across states for a job and have the money, save the hassle of moving yourselves and hiring movers, especially with all the current stress after moving overseas back home. Use your energy for other priorities.

Tip #6: Pets are family. If you have pets, have all the necessary documents as early as possible. Research the requirements for getting your animal out of the country and back to your home country (if not in the U.S.). Generally, start the process at least three to six months in advance, starting with vet appointments to ensure all vaccines are current. Research what flights allow pets to fly by weight and size, and if you take multiple flights, make sure those flights are not codeshare flights since the first flight may allow pets and reserve online, because the remaining leg of flights may have different policies.

Tip #7: You may have limited choices of jobs when moving back to the U.S., so try to be extra flexible about where you end up! Research the locations and workplaces before accepting a job because the ultimate move isn't cheap! Then start planning and preparing before flying back. Also, update your CV or resume and make sure those references are up-to-date.

Tip #8: Get a criminal background check before leaving the country you are departing from, especially if you are getting a new job, particularly in teaching. You will need all the criminal background checks from every country you have lived in. Once you leave that country without getting a criminal background check, it may not be easy since it's easier to be in that country when obtaining the official document. Or, in the worst case, you could contact someone still in that host country to help you or hire a lawyer. Having paper copies of all your background checks will alleviate headaches and relieve stress for your upcoming move.

Tip #9: Learn to budget when moving back to the U.S. There are more hidden costs and other items you may not have to pay while living overseas. Some examples would be car payments, car insurance, gas costs, Uber costs, groceries with added tax, etc. I was shocked about the price of added tax for staying at an Airbnb! Even hotels are now quite pricey, too.

Tip #10: I thought buying a car was already expensive enough, let alone filling up a tank full of gas. Whatever you do, don't lease a vehicle. It's not worth it and is technically not your "own." You will need at least three years to lease a vehicle. In the long run, selling your car is easier when you no longer need it. Remember, to have liquid assets, leasing a car isn't yours! I was considering leasing a car since I knew I would be in the U.S. temporarily and didn't want to have the hassle of going through the car-buying procedure and wiping my hands clean when I sent the car back to the leasing company. However, it was much easier to buy instead of leasing.

Tip #11: Moving furniture overseas, what a pain in the rear! That is why when we moved to another country, we tried to find a place that was already fully furnished. Returning to the U.S. was a slap in the face. How many limited but expensive apartments offer fully furnished places? I suggest saving a lot of money before returning to the U.S. because furniture is costly, even if you find decent second-hand pieces. I purchased a second-hand dining set and an almost brand-new bed frame and mattress set. Our first instinct before buying a used mattress was to search for bed bugs. Once we were in the clear, we bought the mattress. The mattress lasted about two years and I finally purchased a brand-new one, which made a world of difference. I would have gladly spent all the money on a brand new mattress if I had to go back in time when I first moved back home.

Tip #12: Having an unlocked phone is wiser because purchasing a SIM card or an eSIM card and paying as you go is more effortless now. I looked into other cellular services, but they cost at least $80 or more monthly for one line. Boost, Google-Fi, Mint, and more are more affordable than other cellular carriers. I use Mint, and I pay $25 a month for 15GB, and it's sufficient since I am either at home or work, where they already have wifi. The cellular coverage is decent. My 15GB gets me by, and I only use the entire amount if I listen to podcasts daily without downloading them. I recommend purchasing affordable plans if you're not worried about having the best phone plan. If you prefer significant data and more perks, go the more expensive route. It just depends on your preference.

Tip #13: Try to avoid being sucked into the memberships here. There are so many, from beauty products to gym memberships. If you could get by without purchasing these unnecessary memberships, do it. You'll save a ton of money. I got roped into some, spending extra money and wasting it away. I had to look at my budget; the memberships were the first to go, even my Amazon membership. Hey! Prime shipping is fantastic, but if it saves you $15 a month, cut the membership.

Tip #14: Be flexible and open-minded! It takes work to transition back to your home country. You could pick up where you left off, but returning to your motherland is different. My most significant adjustment was to expect to pay more for goods and services than overseas.

Tip #15: Work/Life balance is a huge adjustment when moving back to the States. While living abroad, most teachers leave within an hour of the school day ending to go home to their families or meet friends for dinner or drinks. While living abroad, having a work/life balance was pushed and encouraged, but moving back, corporate America had the opposite mindset. Life is too short, and after collecting stories and tips from other expats, it's a fact that you're easily replaceable. Work to live, not live to work!

. . .

I hope you found these tips useful or helpful if you are moving to the U.S.

Once again, I'm not here to bash my home country but to retell my experiences here and my overseas adventures. After living in the United States, I still adjust to daily tasks and necessities. I can't believe how fast time has flown by because it felt like yesterday that we were driving from Florida to Texas with our entire life in the back of a U-haul truck.

Returning to the States, the honeymoon phase of my reverse culture shock lasted about six months. I was excited to be able to buy all the things I wanted, decorate my place with decorations for the fall and winter seasons, and see my family with a short flight away. Then, my honeymoon phase officially ended, and I entered the next step of the phase called culture shock. After two years, I have passed the recovery stage and am currently at the adjustment stage of reverse culture shock. It's like, "I'm here and going to stay here for a bit longer than planned and just going to have to accept what it is." The acceptance was the most challenging part for me because I wasn't letting go of my grasp of daydreaming of moving back overseas.

There are advantages and disadvantages to living in the United States and the advantages and disadvantages of living abroad. It depends on the day. Some days are worse than others.

Would I want to move back abroad? For sure! But it's not the right timing.

I wrote this book to share my experiences, along with others who had similar ones. If you're reading this and had the same experiences, remember you're not alone! Many days are tough, while other days are easy, and other days, you feel like you're on autopilot. Every so often, you wish you were still the one visiting back home for a short few weeks and then flying back to your host country to continue living your overseas adventure.

I started writing this book in November 2021 and finally finished it. Even though the book is complete, I'm sure I can think of other scenarios and situations I or other people have experienced since living in the States, but I wanted to set a date to finish and publish this book. There's no greater feeling than seeing your work get published. Should I write a sequel to this book or a similar book if I moved back overseas? I'm not sure.

Firstly, I want to extend my heartfelt gratitude to everyone who contributed to this book—the individuals who shared their repatriation stories, who was part of my book launch, the experts who read my work and offered insights, and the readers who joined me on this journey. Secondly, I thank my husband, friends, family, and colleagues who provided their unwavering support and understanding throughout my repatriation journey.

If you would love to share your experiences with me about your repatriation journey, please email me at lotusandhaute@gmail.com and add the subject line: My Repatriation Story. I would love to connect with you.

There is one more piece of advice I could give before I finish with my final thoughts—Life is too short. I realized that if you have a dream to achieve, it's time to take the given steps to acquire that dream. If you are curious about taking the chance to move abroad, reach out to me. I hope to build a community of other repatriates who would also love to contribute their thoughts and advice. That will be my next goal after publishing this book.

It's also about living in the moment; even though I miss my past experiences of the host countries I've previously resided in and have created nothing but lifetime memories. Yet, I'm grateful to live happily in this current chapter of mine.

As I conclude this book, I want to emphasize that the repatriation journey is ongoing. I hope this book serves as a source of empathy, inspiration, and humor for those who find themselves on a similar path. I look forward to the stories and the adventures that lie ahead.

About the Author

Amy Perrier-Morin was born and raised in the United States. She has been an educator for the last twelve years.

Amy's journey in education has been nothing but a globe-trotting adventure. Her teaching career has taken her to the energetic classrooms of China, the vibrant streets of Vietnam, the historical relics of Egypt, and the diverse student populations of the United States.

Beyond the classroom, Amy is an avid traveler. She enjoys discovering new destinations, trying exotic cuisines, and immersing herself in cultures she encounters.

Over the past few years, Amy has been honing her French language skills, a testament to her commitment to personal growth and to connect with others. Her recent journey to South America has ignited her passion to study Spanish, driving her to become multilingual.